Jesus The Revolutionary-

A Chronological Narrative of the Life of Christ From The Virgin Birth to the Samaritan Woman

By John Mol

Matt,

God Bless you as you serve HIS KINGDOM!

Sincerly,

John 8:12

Chapters

Preface

Preface

Asia Minor, or modern day Turkey, has long found significance in being the land bridge that connects the continents of Europe and Asia together. In the decade of the 90s AD, another "bridge" existed in Asia Minor. This bridge was not a geographical location of manmade structure, but rather a man-the Apostle John. The last living apostle, he carried out his final years in Ephesus, serving as bishop to all the churches in Asia Minor. A This historically significant era is immensely important to Christianity. The New Testament was completed and church leaders were being led by the Holy Spirit. As the first century neared its end, the Apostle John was the last man on earth who had actually walked and talked with Jesus, was a follower of Jesus, and was loved by Jesus face-to-face. Following the Resurrection and ascension of Jesus into heaven, the early church looked to the apostles for guidance, direction, teaching and authority. The Apostle John was the last link, the last chain-the last bridge-to the earthly mission and ministry of Jesus Christ.

While the events are both biblically based and historically reliable, this book is a fictional narrative of the words I envision the "beloved disciple" spoke as he talked to the next generation of leaders, most famously the Apostolic Fathers and giants of the faith Polycarp and Papias. As the first century comes to a close, rather than waiting patiently for his life on earth to be extinguished, despite his elderly age, the Apostle John productively mentored, instructed, and educated young men to become the next generation of leaders while fulfilling his duties as Bishop of Ephesus. One such disciple, Polycarp, was born approximately 69 A.D. [B] Subsequently, Polycarp would eventually be appointed as bishop of Smyrna [C] (also modern day Turkey). John's influence is evident as Polycarp emerges in the early church as a leader, writer, defender against heretical teachings, and ultimately becomes a martyr at the age of 86 in approximately 155 A.D. [D]

Historically and chronologically we see an unbroken link through the first two centuries as John becomes an apostle of Jesus prior to becoming bishop of Ephesus. John then mentors Polycarp who eventually becomes bishop of Smyrna. Subsequently, Polycarp influences Irenaeus, who becomes bishop of Lyon (in modern day France) in 177 A.D. Irenaeus is described as, "the first great systematic theologian of the church." [E] Irenaeus gives further credibility to John being the author of the Gospel, which bears his name, when he writes, "John, the disciple of the LORD who reclined on his breast and himself issued the Gospel at Ephesus." [F] In the

2nd and 3rd century a theologian from Alexandria named Clement stated in his book *Hypotyposes* that John wrote a "Spiritual Gospel" to supplement the external facts as written in the other Gospels. [G] Evidence grows as a result that the Apostle John is the author of the Gospel of John. Consequently, John not only authors the deepest gospel theologically, he teaches Polycarp whose writings stress "corrective theology." Polycarp then influences Irenaeus, who, historically, is foundationally paramount for the implementation of systematic theology. Jesus disciples John, John trains Polycarp, and Polycarp influences Irenaeus is a chain of approximately 170 years from the ministry of Jesus Christ to the end of the second century.

Since Irenaeus was born about three decades after the death of the Apostle John, our conversation centers on the elder apostle teaching and relaying the events of his life to Polycarp and Papias, two of his most historically famous and accomplished disciples. The preserved writings of Polycarp show us first hand they were used to combat the heretical teachings of their day. Papias, like his mentor the Apostle John, was a writer. Papias wrote five books that were quoted by early church fathers. [H] While only fragments of his writings have been preserved, these fragments are historically invaluable. Papias' writings include historical events, which add to our knowledge of the some of the events early church not found in the New Testament. After his time with the Apostle John is completed, Papias will go on to become bishop of Hierapolis [1] in Phrygia, which is also in modern day Turkey.

J.D.G. Dunn stated, "In a real sense the history of Christological controversy is the history of the church's attempt to come to terms with John's Christology-first to accept it, then understand and re-express it. The latter task will never end." [J] This is my attempt to re-express this most important of all truths. Here is how I visualize the Apostle John would have told the story of Jesus through his own eyes to his own disciples based on historical facts. This is the account of a first-century Galilean named John and how he witnessed the ministry of Jesus Christ. This is a series which will ultimately narrate, in chronological order, the ministry of Jesus Christ as revealed through Scripture. Subsequent books in the series will continue to analyze the ministry of Jesus Christ in sequential order all leading up to the events of the Passion week including The Triumphal Entry, Crucifixion on the Cross and Resurrection.

In this first book we will analyze the following:

- Events prior to Jesus' birth

- Early life of Jesus
- The ministry of His forerunner John the Baptist
- The baptism and temptation of Jesus
- The calling of the first disciples
- The first miracle at Cana
- The first cleansing of the Temple
- His conversation with Nicodemus and the Samaritan woman

These historical events reveal Jesus as a Revolutionary. They explore how the son of a carpenter from the least respected town of Galilee became the most talked about man in all of Palestine in short period of time. Jesus didn't have in-depth rabbinical training; He was born into poverty, had no earthly possessions, and yet radically took on the religious and political establishments through His teachings and signs unlike anyone in history. Jesus did not fit the description of a Pharisee, Sadducee, Essene, Zealot, Herodian, or any other descriptive term for the Jewish people of that day. Now, nearly 2,000 years after His ministry on earth began, His Kingdom still endures. This is the story of the Revolutionary start of the ministry of Jesus Christ as I envision was told by His "Beloved Apostle."

Chapter 1

Prologue

Setting the Scene

Civilizations rise and fall, but what remains constant is that individuals of their day strive to make their mark in history. Superiors in rank are remembered in the annals of history through the shedding of their inferiors' blood. Historically, it seems that too much attention focuses on the "glory of the battlefield" when the dialogue and conversations were the underlying forces behind the rise and fall of kingdoms.

Fascinating dialogue occurred between Roman General Scipio Africanus and Hannibal Barca of Carthage, prior to their final battle as foes during the Second Punic War. In a conversation between two opposing military leaders, Hannibal personally ranked himself as the third greatest military commander of all time behind Alexander of Macedonia and the Greek General Pyrthus of Epirus. ᴬ This despite losing to Scipio in combat. Perhaps pride kept Hannibal from ranking Scipio, the man who would beat him on the battlefield, ahead of himself historically. Historical outcomes of the battlefield give us conclusions, but the conversation between the two combatants Scipio and

Hannibal adds to the heart of the story of the Second Punic War and gives faceless characters personality and intrigue.

Over a century and a half later, we see the conclusion of the life of another great Roman General, whose final place in perceived historical immortality will not be based on what takes place on a battlefield, but rather in a conversation with the politicians of the Roman Senate. Julius Caesar's legacy was conceivably secure after his victory over Gaul-and his own Roman rival, Pompey-to emerge as the face of the Roman Empire. Whether battling in foreign soil or against his open rival, Julius Caesar reigned supreme; yet it was the hidden foe of quiet conversation among his fellow Romans that would lead to his premature death. Conversation, dialogue, background stories. So much energy focused on the battlefield, but it's the background events and conversations that keep the wheels of change circling into motion.

Hannibal Barca would ultimately lay down his life for no other man, instead choosing to take his own life when faced with the prospect of being hunted down by the Romans while in exile. Julius Caesar would not die for Rome but instead was killed by the Senators of the very empire that he had brought to the heights of power. Glory of the battlefield is personified in the shedding of other men's blood. Life is concluded by drinking poison or twenty-three stab wounds inflicted by Roman senators. Background events tell the story that a battlefield cannot.

With this in mind, let's join a conversation with one of the most influential men of the first century. When hearing of a man of such remarkable influence it is worth noting that he never held a significant military or political title. In fact, his most noteworthy title isn't even as a leader but rather as a follower of Jesus Christ. We join the conversation taking place at the end of the first century in Ephesus as this man, famously known as the Apostle John, is instructing and teaching two young men, Polycarp and Papias, who themselves will rise up to become influential in their own right.

The Apostle John's Words to His Disciples Polycarp and Papias

"*Teknion*" (dear children)[1] everybody has a story. The Roman soldier's training tells the fearless tale of rigidly shaping this methodical warrior's character to embrace being feared over loved for the good of the Roman Empire. The Corinthian sailor spends months at a time facing the terrors of the Mediterranean Sea and in turn justifies the indulgences of sin and pleasure with Corinthians harlots that were so easily accessible. The great highway to the Mediterranean world has taught them tomorrow is not guaranteed, so they justify immorally indulging themselves today. Or the Hebrew widow who survived the Roman onslaught in Jerusalem and now lives her remaining days lonely and haunted by the horrors of the unfathomable bloodshed that she witnessed. She goes about her daily struggles convinced that death will be a comfort. Everybody has a story."

"If I were to tell you my story you might think it is in reference to a Galilean Fisherman. This description would not do my story justice. For the life of a Galilean fisherman is of little interest to you. My story is about a follower of Jesus, and the true essence of my story is found not in the follower but rather in the one being followed. A child was born of a virgin so that God would walk with man once again. Not in the perfection of the Garden of Eden but rather alongside a flawed humanity, marred with selfishness and sin."

"Assuredly, I was privileged to be present in the presence of God in the flesh. With this blessing comes responsibility. What I have witnessed goes against the normalcy of everyday life. Being an eyewitness, along with many others, allowed for the truth of what we experienced to not be dismissed like so many stories of Greek mythology. We have no writings from people who associated with individuals like Hercules, Achilles or Odysseus so the validity of these stories lack credibility. Yet I know what I saw and testified about, and my refusal to renounce my observations lead to my exile on Patmos."

Somberly, the elderly apostle paused before continuing, "and the refusal of my fellow apostles, friends, and even my own brother James, to disown what they have heard, witnessed, and know to be true regarding Jesus Christ, lead to their martyr's death. Yet whether by sword, spear, or crucifixion, they went to their death professing the truth of Jesus Christ our LORD. Jesus claimed to be the Son of God and His ministry, which I witnessed. More so than being my story, this is His story, the story of Jesus Christ, our Savior and King, and I am His eyewitness."

"By the grace of God, He has enabled me to remain to pass on what I have seen and learned to you. When Emperor Domitian exiled me to Patmos, most presumed that the power of Rome was supreme and that decrepit island would be my final resting place. God showered His grace upon me allowing me to visually lay eyes upon my Resurrected LORD once again. God then delivered me from Patmos and installed me into the service at the church of Ephesus for my final days, in the year Trajan became the Emperor of Rome. [B]

"As I shared to open my first epistle, 'That which was from the beginning, which we have heard, which we have seen with our eyes, which we have looked at and our hands have touched-this we proclaim concerning the Word of Life' (I John 1:1 ESV). What I have seen with my own eyes took place about seventy years ago. As the youngest of the disciples of Jesus, all the others have passed from this life before me, and I am the only one left. So listen closely Polycarp and Papias, [C] for there are many battles you must face. These battles are against those who do not teach the truth of the Gospel, but rather man-made theology. Gnosticism has become a great enemy of the church in which false teachers are preaching that which is not inspired by God, but rather proclaimed by man. Polycarp, my son, combat there heretical teachings. [D] Papias, my son, there will be those who doubt the authenticity of my words, as well as the writings of the other apostles. Your role in church leadership will be of great influence and your writings will historically support the claims of Scripture and will further testify what we have written is true." [E]

Early Lives of Jesus and the Apostle John

"Many people have their lives practically planned out for them at birth. If you are the oldest prince in your family, then you will someday be king. If your father is a great military leader, then the mindset typically is you are destined to follow in his footsteps. While I was not born into a household of royalty or military prowess, I, along with my brother James, was destined to sail the sea of Galilee as a fisherman!

"Very impressive" Polycarp chimed in smiling.

"You are a true warrior of the fishing boat my Bishop" stated Papias.

"Sarcasm duly noted *Teknion* (little/dear children)", smiled the elderly Apostle. "Maybe being a fisherman didn't have the prestige of royalty or the glory associated with military success, but let me tell you, nothing struck fear in the hearts of the fish of the Sea of Galilee like the sardines, barbels, or the tilapia as a son of Zebedee. Understandably, the exploits of being a fisherman in Galilee was not awe-inspiring. Galilee was despised by many of the elite in Judea, particularly those from Jerusalem. [F] Perhaps being labeled in this manner is what fueled the "rebel" spirit of so many Galileans, including myself. Galileans abhorred being viewed as "second class" in the eyes of Judeans. Even our accent and dialect was belittled by them.

"Well, apostle as your favorite pupil, I just wanted to say that I find manner of speech endearing" stated Polycarp in light hearted flattery.

"Well thank you my son, but no premier Rabbi shared your sentiment or was interested in taking me on as a pupil, which meant in the eyes of the scholarly I would live out my days as an "unlearned and ignorant man."[2] [G] All signs pointed towards me living out my days continuing the legacy of the family fishing business. All signs except for the one major factor, and this is the will of God. As it turns out, this is the only sign that mattered."

"In preparation for my true calling of being a follower of Jesus Christ I lived and worked with my family in a town right next to Capernaum named Bethsaida.[3] [H] This was on the northeast end of the Sea of Galilee. [I] Under the rule and leadership of Philip the tetrarch, one of Herod I sons, Bethsaida was the beneficiary of architectural and building improvements and as a result the residency increased in large quantities. [J] Herod I, also referred to as "the Great", distinguished himself as the standard bearer for great architectural achievement in ancient Palestine. Herod's building projects include Caesarea Maritima along the shore of the Mediterranean Sea and the desert fortress of Masada. Yet Herod's greatest accomplishment was unparalleled magnificence of The Temple at Jerusalem. Despite these successes, his governance as a harsh tyrannical ruler defines his legacy. Of his three sons who inherited his divided kingdom, Philip the Tetrarch, who ruled for 38 years, was the preferable option to have as a ruler. [K] While Philip the Tetrarchs building exploits failed to match those of his father, transforming our hometown of Bethsaida was the aspect of his rule that most influenced our family.[4]

Bethsaida, like Capernaum, is a fisherman's town. They were just a few miles apart from each other and Bethsaida literally means "house of fishing" [L] which goes to show fishing wasn't a leisurely pastime but a way of life. My father Zebedee loved to joke, "why don't you boys go fishing" as if our inherited occupation should be considered more luxurious than labor. My mother always laughed at the "comedic genius" of my father. My brother and I never did. It's been well over half a century since I heard one of my father's jokes. I miss him, and I miss his jokes. In retrospect, I am extremely appreciative of my upbringing. My father was a man of influence and respected for his business practices. People knew me for who my father was, and being known for who I was associated with has been a recurring theme in my life. Whether it was James, Peter, John the Baptist, or most importantly Jesus, my role was typically secondary.

"You are last Apostle on earth", interjected Papias, "you are playing a secondary role no longer" to which Polycarp nodded in approval.

John then added, "My sons, my time as an apostle taught me that I am to live my life in a secondary role to Christ. Being secondary isn't an insult, it's my calling. Let me share more about the events that led me to become a disciple."

Travel

"Despite the cultural divide between Judeans and Galileans, our neighbors south of Samaria wanted fish from the Sea of Galilee and my father, ever the businessman, was happy to oblige. In fact, our business had some elite customers, none more recognizable than the families of the high priests.[5 N] Our family had a house in Jerusalem so that our business could be profitable on both ends of Palestine. Travelling to Jerusalem whether observing Jewish festivals or for the family business helped shape my life. In fact, historically travel, trade and conquest have shaped society and culture. Civilizations trading, wars, exile, cultures have been shaped by their own travel as well as the travel and conquest of others. Armies would travel out to war. Cities and towns would send out their young men to fight. Everyone knew that death was a possibility for all, probability for many, and for some it seemed that death was almost a certainty. In Ancient Sparta, the story was told of a Spartan mother by the name of Argileonis. Her son Brasidas was an officer for Sparta in the Peloponnesian War. During a battle on the coast of Thrace, Brasidas led the Spartans to victory but ultimately lost his life in the process. When reports were brought back to his mother, Argileonis heard accounts of his admirable death, and, to comfort her, they shared that he was the "best of all Spartans." To this Argileonis replied, "Sirs, my son was a good and honorable man, but Sparta has many a man better than he." O

When it came to the battlefield, nobody had higher expectations for their soldiers than Sparta had for their warriors. Yet Sparta's best fell glaringly short of what heaven had to offer. Perhaps there was some debate whether Brasidas really was the best that Sparta had to offer, but there is no debating that Jesus was the very best that heaven had to give. When Jesus travelled from heaven to come to earth for the greatest battle that would ever be engaged, the battle for eternity, death wasn't a possibility or even a probability. For heaven's favorite Son, death was the plan and a perfect life was His responsibility in the battle for our souls. I have imagined the scene in heaven to be a somber one when they sent off the beloved Son of God. When a family sends a son off to war the home never seems complete in their absence, and I have to imagine that to God the Father, God the Spirit, and the angels in heaven, when Jesus left the indescribable glory of heaven for the humility and degradation of a manger in a stable, heaven felt incomplete. Jesus travelling from heaven to earth did more than just change society and culture. Heaven's finest came to earth to change eternity.

Papias then spoke up, "Bishop, what about Nazareth? You have yet to mention this town. "What about it?" stated John. "Nazareth was so insignificant practically every Galilean family never even brought it up. "So your family didn't mention Nazareth then?" asked Polycarp "I said practically every Galilean family" stated John as he smiled wryly. "Our home was a rare exception. Nazareth did not make it to the dinner conversations of many Galilean households   and was well on its way to not even being mentioned as a footnote in history. Nazareth was too small and insignificant for any businesses in Capernaum to want to make the 20 plus mile trek. Yet in Nazareth lived the family of my uncle Joseph and Aunt Mary.[6] "Let's go back to events prior to my birth. My mother was very young when her older sister Mary was engaged to be married to the man who would become my Uncle Joseph, and the adopted father of Jesus.[7]

"This engagement was nothing special or unique. Joseph and Mary's opinion mattered little up to this point, and their parents arranged for the engagement. As was custom of this day, it was not even necessary for the couple to meet prior to them becoming engaged. [P] Step two in the process of getting married is known as the betrothal period. Here is where the originators of this tradition found it wise for an engaged couple to meet prior to marriage."

"Actually meeting your spouse is a key component for long term marital success," stated Polycarp jokingly.

"True," stated the loving Apostle without giving much attention to the attempted humor of his pupil prior to continuing. "Now if the woman decided not to get married, this was the time she would have to make that choice. What was evident to my Aunt Mary from the start is that while my Uncle Joseph would not accumulate worldly wealth, he was rich in character. Not only would Mary accept the choice of Joseph as her husband, but he was chosen by God to be the earthly father figure to God the Son. Oh, the conversations we had in her last years", stated John softly, recollecting discussions he had with his Aunt Mary after taking her into his home as if she were his own mother (John 19:27). "She used to reminisce of the simplicity of being a teenager living in the hills of Southern Galilee, while waiting to be married properly to Joseph. Then, through an act of the Holy Spirit Jesus was conceived (Luke 1:35). Every act ever done by man, every Pyramid Egypt ever built, every lesson Aristotle ever taught, every battle Julius Caesar ever fought, every road Rome ever paved, pales in comparison to the miraculous conception of a Galilean teenager named Mary."

"Our Savior was therefore not born under the curse of sin like all men born from Adam,"[8] remarked Polycarp sharing a theological lesson taught to him by the Apostle John.

Papias added, "How your family must have rejoiced knowing God used Joseph and Mary in His plan of redemption.

John shook his head in a dejected manner as he thought of how Mary and Joseph were perceived by neighbors, by friends, by family. "My fellow Apostle Matthew truthfully stated my Uncle Joseph was a 'righteous man' (Matthew 1:19). "However, he was not viewed by his community or even own family in this manner."

"Why?" a confused Papias asked. "He was obedient to God and never violated the sanctity of marriage."

"Innocence before God historically has often meant guilty in the court of public opinion. Before I was ever rejected and exiled by the Roman Empire, before John the Baptist was rejected by the authority of Herod Antipas, or before the rejection of our LORD led to his crucifixion, Joseph was rejected by his community and even his family for the act of adultery he never committed" the apostle responded. "This pattern began historically with Abel and continues in the lives of Noah, the Patriarchs, Moses, David, and the prophets. In the early church it is seen with Stephen, James the brother of Jesus, Peter, Paul, and my dear brother James. Yet, in the course of human history, nowhere was this more evident than when God the Father accepted the sacrifice of atonement by his only begotten Son, Jesus Christ, while men not only rejected His message but tortured and crucified the Righteous Lamb of God."

Silence among those present allowed for the heaviness of the topic to be mentally digested before the Apostle John continued his explanation of the events surrounding Joseph and Mary. "They were considered the 'black sheep' of the family. They were condemned as adulterers by society and 'second rate' by their own family. Economically, they were several notches below my parents Zebedee and Salome. Socially, people have justified an aura of superiority for practically anything. Joseph and Mary lived there lives in humility and righteousness rather than self-exaltation. Societies would do well to emulate their character."

"They were nothing but obedient despite being judged unfairly in the court of public opinion. After the birth of our Savior Jesus Christ, my Uncle Joseph and Aunt Mary showed proper reverence to the law of Moses and brought a sacrifice to the Temple (Leviticus 12:6-8). Poverty designated them unable to offer a lamb on behalf of their son, so a pair of doves or pigeons sufficed. Walking into the area of The Temple known as the "Court of Women" Mary made her way to the thirteen chests or "trumpets", which was the designation for monetary contributions to the Temple. Trumpet III was designated for payment for turtledoves and Trumpet IV for pigeons. ^{Q} Mary took the humble walk of a poor, young mother to offer the simple sacrifice on behalf of her son."

Insignificant offering in the eyes of the priests who were on duty, for no significant woman walks to Trumpet III. Mary's offering on behalf of her son was ignored by the masses but received by God. God wisely gave the role of being the adoptive father to my Uncle Joseph. Josephs' riches are not found not in worldly wealth but rather in the righteousness of

God. Unquestionably, the church in every age would do well to strive to emulate this characteristic.

Jesus Being About His Father's Business

Luke 2:41-52[9]

"Apostle", stated Papias "how could your family not recognize earlier that Jesus was the Messiah?"

"My child", stated John, "Prior to my own birth my family recognized my cousin Jesus was unique at an early age. Numerous times I heard this story recounted. My older brother James was a newborn and my only existence was in the foreknowledge of God. It was Spring and the time of Passover was upon us. My parents and my Uncle Joseph and Aunt Mary were good Galileans. Being faithful to the Hebrew tradition and law of Moses, they travelled to Jerusalem to celebrate Passover and the Feast of Unleavened Bread (Exodus 23:14-15, Leviticus 23:4-8, Deuteronomy 16:1-8; 16-17). Annually, this is the first of three great festivals to be observed by the Jewish people, [R] along with the Feast of Weeks and the Feast of Tabernacles. Joseph and Mary were devout in their obedience to Hebrew Law and Tradition and sincere in their worship of God. One particular Sabbath when Jesus was twelve, He and his family made the journey from Nazareth down to Jerusalem. This caravan that left Nazareth together met up with my parents and others from our community."

"Jerusalem was unbelievably chaotic during Passover as multitudes of people would travel from even outside Judah and Galilee to worship during this week. [S] Groups would travel on the road east of the Jordan River in large numbers to protect themselves from thieves and robbers.

"For there is strength in numbers", stated Polycarp confidently.

"There is my child. These large numbers also increase the likelihood of not recognizing when somebody is missing, like for example, your own son.[10] Being twelve was a transitional age for a Jewish boy, for they would be considered a "son of the law." [T] Once the week was over and the multitude began their journey back, Jesus stayed behind, in a place where He felt most at home, in the Temple, speaking of the things of God. As the day of travelling was coming to an end, Mary surveyed the scene and noticed one person wasn't accounted for and asked the obvious question to her husband, 'Where is Jesus?' Their assumption that Jesus would be among others in his own age was incorrect. [U] A frantic search by friends and family lead them to the undesirable conclusion, Jesus was left in Jerusalem. Regrettable how often Jesus is forgotten by society as he was by his own family. Joseph and Mary spent a whole day backtracking, and it wasn't until the third day that Jesus was found.

"The third day" stated Papias with Polycarp nodding his head in approval.

"Yes, my sons", Jesus was absent and again became visible to those who loved Him on the third day. This powerful image of symbolism should not be lost on us or future believers as well.

In Hindsight, perhaps the first place that Joseph and Mary should have searched is the Temple. Arriving at the last place they could think of, there was Jesus, sitting in the Temple courts speaking to the most brilliant Jewish Rabbis of that day and astounding everyone with his knowledge. Once Joseph and Mary saw Him, they rushed over to Him. Any parent who has lost a child can relate to the wave of emotions that swept over Mary at that time. She was relieved, joyful, frustrated, angry, and confused. "Son, why have you treated us like this?" Never had Jesus done anything that could be viewed as disobedient or rebellious and Mary was as frustrated as she was grateful to have found Him. Jesus, even at his young age, was cognitive of his calling when He calmly stated that "It was necessary"[11] for Him to be about His Father's business.

On several occasions, Jesus would state when something was "necessary", including His own suffering and death. This conversation stuck with my Aunt Mary. For, while she knew this to be true all along, the realization dawned on her that long before Jesus was ever her son, He was God's. She couldn't be upset that Jesus wasn't entirely focused on his mother's business, He needed to be about His Father's. Ultimately, the purpose of the Temple was for God to dwell with men. While Jesus was speaking to people in the Temple, God was dwelling with men. Despite the anxiety of losing Jesus, it was a wonderful reunion on the third day, and, in retrospect, it is clear Jesus understood His higher calling. This was but a glimpse of the reunion that would take place on another third day, when Jesus appeared to His followers after he conquered death. When Jesus conquered death on our behalf, once again, Jesus was about His Father's business.

Chapter 1 Footnotes

Teknion is a Greek noun that means "little" or "dear children." It is used in an affectionate manner. This Greek noun is used eight times in the New Testament, and every time that it was used the Apostle John was the author. *Teknion* is used once in the Gospel of John (John 13:33) and seven times in I John (I John 2:1; 2:12; 2:28; 3:7; 3:18; 4:4; 5:21).

[2] Peter and John were arrested and taken before the high priests and other religious leaders after healing a crippled beggar while they were in Jerusalem (Acts 3:1-10) and preaching on faith in Jesus (Acts 3:16). that the healing was done through "faith in Jesus" (Acts 3:16). In Acts 4:13 it states that Peter and John were *agrammatos* which means, "unlearned" or "uneducated" which describes the fact that they weren't trained in Rabbinical schools or recognized among Jewish religious circles

[3] Many make the case that James and John were from Bethsaida. We read in John 1:44- "Philip, like Andrew and Peter was from the town of Bethsaida." It makes sense that the Apostle John didn't mention if James and John were also from Bethsaida because he never refers to him or his brother by name in the Gospel of John, only mentions them as "sons of Zebedee." We also read after the first miraculous catch of fish after Peter was done speaking to fish it states in Luke 5:9-10a- "For he and all his companions were astonished at the catch of fish they had taken, and so were James and John, the sons of Zebedee, Simon's partners." Peter and Andrew were probably born in Bethsaida, and then moved to Capernaum as is apparent in the fact that Jesus healed Peter's mother-in-law after He entered into Capernaum and this was done in Peter's house (Matthew 8:5, 14). Capernaum and Bethsaida were right next to each other. Scholars have made cases for James and John being from both Bethsaida and Capernaum.

[4] Josephus describes the building and work done to Bethsaida as making it transition from a village to "the dignity of a city." Subsequently Bethsaida is historically referred to as Bethsaida-Julias, named after Caesar's daughter [M]

[5] Franciscan legend states that Zebedee's family business sold fish to the family of the high priest. This seems all the more credible when reading how John had access to the high priest's courtyard after the arrest of Jesus, because was known by the high priest (John 18:15). Since Peter didn't have access to the high priest's courtyard it appears that while at times the four of them were partners (Luke 5:9-10) it wasn't a complete partnership.

[6] Multiple times in the Gospels we see that Salome is mentioned at the crucifixion scene in Matthew 27:55-56 with Mary the mother of James and Joses (Mary the mother of Jesus) and the mother of Zebedee's sons.

Cross-reference this to John 19:25a- "Near the cross of Jesus stood his mother, his mother's sister." So in Matthew she is referred to as "mother of Zebedee's sons or basically, "the mother of James and John" and in John the woman in reference isn't mentioned by name but rather the sister of Jesus's mother. In Mark 16:1 she is mentioned by name going to the tomb of Jesus

[7] When analyzing the relationship between Mary and Salome, viewing Mary as the older sister is logical when considering the age of their children. While presumably Mary was very young when she gave birth to Jesus, since James and John appear to be significantly younger, probably more than 10 years younger, it is a solid presumption that Salome was younger than Mary. Therefore, events that happened to Joseph and Mary were likely discussed within the family.

[8] Every man that has been born has been born under the curse of sin. We read in Psalm 51:5- "Surely I was sinful at birth, sinful from the time my mother conceived me." David recognized he was born under sin because he comes from sinful man. The Apostle Paul states we inherit sin from Adam when he writes in Romans 5:12- "Therefore, just as sin entered the world through one man, and death through sin, and in this way death came to all men because all me sinned." Jesus Christ was not born under the curse of Adam's sin but rather from a miraculous work of God. His Righteousness is our hope. Paul later states in Romans 5:19- "For just as through the disobedience of the one man the many were made sinners, so also through the obedience of the one man the many will be made righteous."

[9] Zebedee and Salome witnessing this event is not in Scripture but it's based on the combination of historical research and rational that they were possibly they present. Jesus was born prior to the death of Herod the Great. Based on historical research Herod died on April 1, 4 B.C. [N] After the Magi were warned in a dream to go a different route, Herod was furious and ordered to kill all the boys two years old and under (Matthew 2:16). This does not mean that Jesus was two, because Herod would presumably have no problem justifying "rounding up" when figuring out what ages to kill in order to protect his throne according to his own logic. Reason would point that Jesus was not a newborn so guesstimating that the birth of Jesus is 5 B.C. is a reasonable estimate. Luke states that Jesus is twelve years old when his parents took him to the Temple. This makes this approximately 7 A.D. when this event takes place. When figuring the ages of James and John it is understood that James is older since he is always mentioned first. John is typically viewed as the youngest of the twelve and is possibly even a teenager when Jesus first calls him to follow Him in 27 A.D. Therefore, John is not born yet but James might be and Zebedee and Salome would have been reasonably early on in their

marriage. Again, this is speculation but not speculation without cause and analysis.

[10] Scripture states Mary and Joseph traveled with relatives so it's possible if not probable that Mary met up with her sister and brother-in-law for the journey. Since Jesus is significantly older than James and John it is fair to guess that Zebedee and Salome were married by this point but uncertain if James and John were even born at this time. If they were then likely they would have been very young.

[11] In Luke 2:49 Jesus states, "I had to" or "I must be" my Father's house. The Greek verb used is *dei* which means, "it is necessary; inevitable" (biblehub.com). This is the first of 18 times this verb is used in the Gospel of Luke

Chapter 2

Galilean Fishermen, Politics in Judea and Religious Sects

"As I grew into my teenage years, being one of two sons of a father who was running a successful fishing business, my responsibilities were enhanced."

"Is it because your father recognized that you were growing to be a man of great skill and talent?" inquired Papias sincerely.

"No, it was because my father knew that he had to pay his hired workers, but being a son of Zebedee comes with the distinct honor of working for free", stated John in a manner of self-deprecating humor. "As I previously shared, I was given the duty of transporting some of our fish to Jerusalem and Judea to expand the market for our business."

"My father wisely chose Andrew to work with me. Andrew and I were frequently partners when we fished (Luke 5:10a) and now we were partners transporting the fish. Andrew was older and more established than I, yet he was a man of such great character that what bothered other men did not negatively impact him."

"Why do you suppose that is?" stated Papias.

"Because he was unquestionably one of the sincerest and genuine men that I have ever known. Andrew was most fascinated by truth and routinely sought for opportunities for others to benefit. We did share many things in common. We were, of course, both fishermen. Younger brothers often overshadowed by our older siblings, Simon and James respectively. We also felt uneasiness about our current lot in life. What started as a routine business transaction turned into us meeting up with a man whose ministry was the fulfillment of Old Testament prophesies."

"Were you going to see Jesus?" Polycarp asked.

"Not yet" stated John. "We were going to see another who was prophesied about in Scripture. We were going to see John the Baptist."

"Our journey would unexpectedly go from family business to business of God. Economically, Galilee was a very appealing place to live, not only having the benefits of a fresh water lake, but fertile soil for farming allowed for the large population in Galilee to have diversity in their economy. Trade between Galilee and Jerusalem was prominent with Galilean exports ranging from fruit to oil to wine to…

"Fish" interrupted Polycarp brimming with confidence.

The elderly apostle smiled and shook his head amusingly. "I was going to say grape-syrup, [A] but yes, fish both fresh and salted were traded with Jerusalem to which the Zebedee family greatly benefited."

After arriving in Jerusalem, Andrew and I immediately head off towards the residence of the high priest. Our business in Jerusalem started with our most prestigious customer Joseph Caiaphas, the high priest, but he is often referred to simply as Caiaphas. "Is this the same Caiaphas for whom Jesus stood on trial? stated Papias. "Yes, the same Papias known historically for holding trial over Jesus, was one of our family's best customers.[1] [B]

"High priests during this historical era didn't ascend to authority through selfless adherence to the Law of God and by serving God's chosen people. Chief priests routinely manipulated the system for their own benefit. [D] This infuriated many of the Hebrew people, none more so than the Zealots who viewed the aristocratic elite as compromisers, which was often an accurate assessment. Yet the people's opinion was insignificant when it came to who their high priest would be. Joseph Ben Caiaphas became the high priest when Roman Procurator[2] Valerius Gratus appointed him to this position. [E]

"How did Valerius Gratus become Procurator of Judaea?" asked Polycarp.

"He was also appointed, but by Tiberius Caesar." "By Caesar" stated a shocked Polycarp. "So Valerius Gratus appointed Caiaphas to be high priest."

"That is correct Polycarp" said John.

Papias then continued, "and Valerius Gratus was the Procurator because Caesar Tiberius appointed him."

"That is correct Papias" said John as he nodded his head in approval. "So…" the Apostle John raised his eyebrows and turned his head so as to gesture a teacher signaling for his students to finish the connective thought."

"So the spiritual leader of the Jewish people in Jerusalem ultimately was appointed by Rome," answered Polycarp in a quiet tone with Papias just gazing off in the distance as comprehension of the dynamics of the culture from the era of the life of Jesus had begun to settle in.[3]

"How were the people ok with the Roman Government, a pagan culture in which their own ruler, Caesar, accepted worship from his people, indirectly appointed the position of high priest?" asked Papias in candid disbelief.

"I wouldn't be ok with it" stated Polycarp, agreeing with the sentiment of Papias.

"This attitude that you convey was the same disposition held by many" answered John.

"Then why was it accepted" asked Polycarp.

John paused for moment and sat back in his chair and took a deep breath before continuing, "Because, the past several centuries have been filled with turmoil, and many reasoned the current predicament as unfavorable, but avenues of change were hard to come by. Ruling authorities in Palestine were from varied different empires over the last 800 years, but rarely did the descendants of Abraham, the children of Israel, rule themselves. In many ways, the attitude of the people, particularly in Judea, was one of compliance with the ruling political authorities. Unfortunately, the office of the high priesthood often chose not to comply with the commands of God, but justified immoral decisions which were subsequently corrupt. [H] God established the priesthood to be righteous examples and mediators for His people on behalf of Him (Psalm 132:9) Yet Caiaphas and others high priests during Roman rule often chose the pleasures of man over the righteousness of God."

"Teacher, being the young man that you were, how did you feel about how the structural hierarchy in Judea?" Polycarp asked genuinely.

"Well my son," stated the Apostle, "I was in a complicated scenario. I was working for my father who was a Galilean businessman, and Caiaphas the high priest was our customer, and he was a Judean. When I, a Galilean, and Caiaphas, a Judean, were meeting, it had been over 950 years since our regions of origin had been part of the same country, the nation of Israel. Galileans and Judeans had geographic, cultural, and ethnic differences. Finances connected my family to many in Judea, but for the Jews in Galilee who weren't monetarily connected to the Jews in Judea, there was still a bridge. Over the course of a millennium, the Jewish people endured Civil War, foreign rule, oppression, destruction of the Temple, attempted genocide, scattering of the Hebrew people on three continents, and yet the Holy Scriptures and the culture of God's chosen people survived all this. The written Law of Moses, the historical books, books of wisdom, and books of prophecy survived all this. The race of the Jews survived all this, and despite obvious differences between Jewish Galileans and Judeans, we were still connected."

Polycarp proceeded to ask that weighty one-word question. "How?"

"What shall I say in response to this? If God is for us who can be against us?" (Romans 8:31) answered the Apostle John humbly quoting the Apostle Paul.

The Apostle John noticed Papias was struggling to grasp showed fatherly love and intuition and said, "What is it my son?"

Papias, who would himself grow up to become an influential pillar in the early church, struggled to find the words "It's just…"

"Go on" stated John as he listened intently.

"It's so hard for me to fathom people still worshipping YHWH, the sacrificial system and priesthood still in place, the entirety of Scripture, all surviving everything Hebrew people endured over the course of a millennium."

"My child" stated the Apostle John in a compassionate manner proving him worthy of the moniker 'the beloved disciple,' "that's how you know it's of the LORD. It's so difficult to grasp the workings of God through our human minds, because how can the limited grasp He who is limitless? While you can't fathom the depth of His ways or

His knowledge, my child, you also can't grasp the love He has for you," said the former son of thunder, now tenderly speaking to two pupils whom, while he was never a father of sons, he viewed as such. Tears welled up in his eyes as he quoted his divinely inspired first epistle, "How great is the love the Father has lavished on us, that we should be called the children of God! And that is what we are!" (I John 3:1a NIV) Papias and Polycarp were both moved at the emotional shift of the tone during the exchange.

Papias added, "It's just unfathomable to me…almost 1,000 years."

"Almost 1,000 years" said the Apostle John nodded his head in agreement. "Historically it's undeniable and God's sovereign grace through it all is unquestionable."

"So God deserves all the credit?" asked Papias one last time.

"He always does my son", smiled the elderly Apostle as he looked affectionately at Papias, "he always does."

"Now, back to the story of Andrew and I going to Jerusalem. Being from a fishing village in Galilee, every time I saw the archaeological beauty and splendor of the "city of David" I was amazed. From the height of the towers, which were part of the walls, to the beautiful white marble streets, walking up to the city it was abundantly evident, we weren't in Galilee anymore. Jerusalem was built on four hills with Mount Zion being the most famous of the four. In the Northeastern corner of Zion was the location of the palace of the high priest. [J]

Many people presumed that since Caiaphas was the current high priest, he had the most influence in Jerusalem.

"He wasn't?" asked Papias surprisingly.

John shook his head before continuing, "When it came to guidance and direction even Caiaphas looked to Annas." "Jesus was questioned by Annas also before his crucifixion right?" stated Polycarp.

"Yes" John answered, "prior to standing trial before Caiaphas (Matthew 26:57; Mark 14:53; Luke 22:54), Jesus first stood trial before Annas (John 18:19-24). After a 10 year run as high priest (6-15 AD) Annas was removed from power by the Procurator of Judea, Valerius Gratus, three years before Caiaphas was appointed to this position. Annas was also the father-in-law of Caiaphas.[K]

"So his influence was found in being the former high priest as well hierarchy in the most powerful Jewish family in Jerusalem" reasoned Polycarp.

"Precisely" stated the Apostle John.

Papias chimed in with another question, "Was Valerius Gratus the Procurator of Judaea when you and Andrew went to Jerusalem prior to your encounter with John the Baptist?"

John shook his head, "No, Judaea had another Procurator at that time. A man whom I am sure you have both heard of before. His name was Pontius Pilate."

John continued, "At this time Caiaphas, was about halfway through his 18-year run as high priest of Israel.[4] One family had a monopoly on the position of high priest for many years. Joseph Ben Caiaphas was the current high priest but Annas was the patriarch of this priestly dynasty. As the elder statesman in both age and experience he was often called upon for counsel and guidance from those who were part of the Sanhedrin and as well as by his son-in-law. As Andrew and I prepared to complete the business transaction Annas make his way over to Caiaphas in an earnest manner.

"Excuse me, but Caiaphas, I need to speak to you for a moment" Annas said. While the present and former high priest engaged in conversation, Andrew and I decided to eaves drop. "There is a man whose teachings are inspiring a movement" stated Annas to his son-in-law.

Immediately you could see the back of Caiaphas stiffen as he could sense this most recent development was not one that should be taken lightly.

"Is this movement taking place in Jerusalem?" asked Caiaphas.

"No, this movement started in the Judean wilderness and is currently along the banks of the Jordan" affirmed Annas.

"Do we know the name of this man who inspires others to follow him into the wilderness?" asked Annas to the high priest.

"Yes, we do. This man is Zachariah's son John."

"Upon hearing the description I was stunned to come to the realization this "wilderness preacher" was a relative of mine. For just as Mary, the mother of Jesus, was related to Elizabeth, the mother of John, so would my mother Salome, the sister of Mary, be related to Elizabeth. After the dialogue between the former and current high priest, Annas walked away and Caiaphas turned his attention back towards Andrew and I.

"Please forgive me for the interruption" stated Caiaphas. "You didn't travel from Galilee to hear about the ramblings of a wilderness preacher.

"Of course not", stated Andrew, "but at least he won't be any competition for our business. The fishing is terrible out there," stated Andrew getting a laugh from the high priest before he added "Safe journeys home, we will see each other soon."[5]

"After wrapping up our business obligations, Andrew and I decided to see for ourselves this John the Baptist whose following seems to have rattled the religious elite of Jerusalem."

"But wouldn't your father be expecting for you to return to help with the business?" asked Polycarp.

"Of course, but you see, I was a Galilean, and Galileans were known to be "impulsive and passionate" [M]

"But wasn't he still expecting you? Wasn't he concerned your impulsiveness leaving would hurt the family business?" Polycarp prodded further.

"He was very understanding, after all, he was a Galilean too" smiled John. "For Galileans, honor was more valuable than money." [6 N] While my father cared greatly about the success and growth of the family fishing business, pursuing knowledge and truth justifiably took precedence and subsequently a few more fish would find refuge in the Sea of Galilee for a bit longer.

"If your father was upset though", Papias continued, "were you ready for that?"

"What can I say" smiled John, "I was impulsive."

"Based on what we heard John the Baptist was preaching and baptizing by Bethany. This wasn't the Bethany where Lazarus, Martha, and Mary lived. Our dear friends lived only two miles from Jerusalem. This Bethany was beyond the Jordan River (John 1:28), on the eastern side of the River.[7] We had to travel to the Jordan Valley, south of Jericho. [Q] Here the Jordan River was well known location where the water in the river was shallow and would allow for people and animals to be able to cross."

"Prior to his baptismal ministry John the Baptist lived in isolation in the challenging terrain of the Judean Wilderness. Imagine living in intense heat, longing for a cool breeze of refreshment. Then the southeast wind would blow a stifling heat [R] causing your situation to be even more uncomfortable and unbearable. Day after day gazing upon sand and dried up grass to remind John of the unforgiving nature the wilderness had to offer. Even the sky wasn't a refreshing blue but rather the appearance of brass. Thorn bushes that were hampered from reaching their optimal height due to the scarcity of water was a frequent image. Snakes and scorpions were our John's only companions. [5] Yet the wilderness experience was vital for John's ministry because the penetrating heat and extreme isolation strengthened him to endure the opposition he would face from religious and political leaders of Palestine."

"As we travelled I leaned upon the wisdom and knowledge of my older and wiser companion Andrew. "Who do you think John the Baptist is religiously connected too?" I asked. Andrew looked down as we walked and fixated upon the question. Andrew has repeatedly shown himself to be a consistently reliable source to answer my varied questions, but this time appeared to be as baffled as I was.

Shrugging his shoulders, he stated, "That's the same question that has me baffled" as he verbalized the reasons John the Baptist didn't appear to be a Sadducee, Pharisee, or Essene. "I don't see how he could be a Sadducee because Caiaphas and Annas are both Sadducees and it doesn't make sense for them to be in the dark about the teachings and work of a fellow Sadducee."

Then I added, "Not to mention the Sadducees are typically more focused on wealth and political power. What would a

Sadducee find alluring about isolating himself in the barren, desolate wilderness?"

"Exactly", Andrew stated.

"Could he be a Pharisee?" I asked sincerely."

"Mmmmmm….. again, it doesn't fit" Andrew said while shaking his head but also showing the look of uncertainty on his face. "Pharisees like to be among the people and increase their influence. You expect an influential Pharisee to rise from the teachings of the synagogues and under a prominent Rabbi and it doesn't appear that the ministry of John is a product of this system.

"Could he be an Essene?" I asked. "After all, the Essenes are in the wilderness."

"You're right John" Andrew answered, "the Essenes are in the wilderness. However, they are part of communities and John the Baptist appears to be operating independently."

"We would also find out later that the diet of John the Baptist excluded him from being an Essene. For the Essenes took a vow to abstain from eating flesh, fish, and locusts. [U] John the Baptist received his physical nourishment by consuming locusts and wild honey (Matthew 3:4). So out of these three options John the Baptist didn't fit any of them. His economic and political status showed him not to be a Sadducee. His geographic location and message showed him not to be a Pharisee, and his solidarity showed him not to be an Essene. As we analyzed how our process of elimination worked, it appeared that we had eliminated all of the options.

"Apostle", Papias interjected. "It has been almost three decades since the Temple has been destroyed.[8] You lived through the time when the Pharisees, Sadducees, and Essenes were all relevant and their ideology was discussed and debated. As a result of the Jewish Revolt against Rome (AD 66-74) aspects of Jewish culture which took place prior to the revolt ceased to exist. Since you lived extensively prior to the revolt, could you further elaborate on the differences?"

"Absolutely Papias. Each of these three groups shared the belief the true understanding that Judaism would reveal to the world there is only one God, it seems that is where most of their similarities ended."

"When it came to who was most popular among the masses, Pharisees had the greatest following by a wide margin.

"So could they sway the opinions of the people when they spoke out about a topic or an issue that impacted the people?" asked Polycarp. "

Without question this was the case" stated the Apostle John. "If the Pharisees spoke out against the acting high priest or even a king or ruler that was appointed by Rome, then the people typically accepted and supported this view. [V] Altogether there were about 6,000 Pharisees [W] and this group swayed the opinion of the masses more than any other religious sect."

"So the Pharisees were the most powerful of the three groups right Apostle?" stated Polycarp.

"Well, they were the most influential among the people, but when it came to political power and wealth, neither of the other two religious sects came even close to the authority wielded by the Sadducees. They were an aristocratic group of priests who first gained power when, after the exile, a Persian king gave them the authority to oversee and maintain the Temple. [X] With the power, given to them by the political ruling authorities, they would push the agenda that maintaining the Temple was of primary importance in order for the children of Israel to hold on to their culture as well as allow them to have a strong relationship with God."

Papias chimed in, "Did they desire for the nation of Israel to be a free and self-governing nation once again?"

"Well, considering that for the last few centuries they had significant power entrusted to them by the foreign nations that governed Palestine, they weren't eager to start a revolution with Rome."

"Which wasn't a popular decision among the people I would imagine" said Polycarp.

"You are correct my son" answered John, "It was evident that the Sadducees did what many ruling authorities have done in the past and I am sure will do in the future, and that is exchange popularity for power."

"Now on to the Essenes who weren't 'popular' like the Pharisees or 'powerful' like the Sadducees, but they appeared to be the most 'purposeful' in how they approached each day. Essenes were always Jewish by birth but an Essene by choice. [BB] Essenes viewed pleasure as evil and virtue as their primary objection. Being an Essene require an extraordinary amount of devotion to fulfill their requirements. Many Essenes chose not to marry to avoid quarrels and arguments and they wouldn't have servants so as to avoid even potentially acting in an unrighteous manner. [CC] They would get up in the morning before sunrise and prior to saying even a word they would offer up prayers to God that they would receive from their forefathers. [DD]

"They had very different goals didn't they?" asked Polycarp.
"They did", John affirmed, "on one extreme, the Sadducees
sought after and acquired wealth, in the other extreme, the
Essenes shared their wealth in such a way so as to ensure that
nobody was wealthy and nobody was in poverty but they
were all economically equal. EE Sadducees oversaw the daily
operations of the Temple but the Essenes wouldn't send
offerings to the Temple because they thought the Temple was
corrupt and they believed their own method was purer." FF

"There goals and actions were as diverse as their view of
God's intervention in their lives. For starters, the Essenes
believed everything that happens to them has already been
predetermined by God and is all connected to fate. GG
"Everything?" asked Polycarp.
"Everything!" affirmed the Apostle John.
"So they would view that the fact that the Essenes
themselves were a group of people who formed their own
rules and standards apart from the Temple" stated Papias.
"Predetermined by God" affirmed John.
"How about the fact that they viewed the actions of the
Sadducees as morally corrupt" expressed Polycarp.
"Also predetermined by God" confirmed the Apostle. "Of the
three religious sects of Judaism at this time, the Essenes were

the only who believed everything was connected to fate. The Pharisees were in the middle, believing that some actions were connected to fate and some actions weren't predetermined. Meanwhile the Sadducees believed that there was no such thing as fate, nothing is predetermined and the individual is credited with their successes and responsible for the shortcomings."

"So they gave no glory to God for their successes?" Papias stated, a bit surprised considering they were entrusted with overseeing the Temple.

"My son, think of the words of our Savior Jesus Christ when he said, 'I tell you the truth, it is hard for a rich man to enter the kingdom of heaven. Again, I tell you, it is easier for a camel to go through the eye of a needle than for a rich man to enter the kingdom of God' (Matthew 19:23-24). Sadducees had the power and the prestige. They were part of an aristocracy that owned wealth and land. [HH] If they were to give credit to God for their wealth and success, then that means they deserve less credit themselves. Sadly the Sadducees were often blinded by the desire for their version of success. They didn't want to be identified as merely devoted worshippers of YHWH with fellow Jewish brethren. They wanted to be esteemed as Jews with an elevated position within the control of the dominant Roman Empire. [II]

This desire impacted their theology, inhibited their focus of pure and genuine worship of the LORD, and deviated their efforts on earthly riches because there was no heavenly gain."

"No heavenly gain?" said Papias in a perplexed manner.

"Not in their minds, not in their teachings, and certainly not based on their actions" stated the aged Apostle. "For the Sadducees didn't believe or accept that there was any life after this life or any supernatural act of intervention from God. Sadducees didn't believe in the Resurrection of the dead or even in angels or spirits (Mark 12:18, Acts 23:8).

Papias, surprised as this revelation pertaining to the Sadducees, asked, "What about the words in the book of Daniel, "But at that time your people-everyone whose name is found written in the book-will be delivered. Multitudes who sleep in the dust of the earth will awake: some to everlasting life, others to shame and everlasting contempt" (Daniel 12:1b-2 NIV)

"Or the prophet Hosea", chimed in Polycarp, "when the LORD spoke to him and said, 'I will ransom them from the power of the grave, I will redeem them from death'" (Hosea 13:14)

"Or the prophet Isaiah when he declared the promise of a 'new heavens and a new earth' (Isaiah 66:22) Papias stated in a clearly agitated manner as these two disciples of the Apostle John were making a Scriptural case for the argument against the theology of the Sadducees. Sensing that their passion and anger was rising rapidly and perhaps seeing similarities from his youth, the Apostle took on the role of elder statesman, and simply raised his right hand calmly in the air having a tranquil impact on Polycarp and Papias.

 John, looking at his two young protégés, let out a broad grin and stated, "Your passion for truth is encouraging, and may your thirst for knowledge never wane. Scripture is abundantly clear about judgment after death and the gift of eternal life to those whom belong to the LORD. Nehemiah described how the multitudes in heaven worshipped the LORD (Nehemiah 9:6). While the Sadducees claimed only the books of Moses had any authority [JJ] even Moses wrote of these heavenly beings, "The LORD came from Sinai and dawned over them from Seir; He shone forth from Mount Paran. He came with myriads of holy ones [9], from the south, from His mountain slopes" (Deuteronomy 33:2). Additionally, a cherubim was placed to guard the Garden of Eden after Adam and Eve were banished (Genesis 3:24). God has revealed the truth of angels through His Holy Word. Yet sadly the Sadducees justified denying their existence."[10]

John then transitioned from Biblical evidence to personal experience when he stated, "While suffering through loneliness and isolation on the island of Patmos, God revealed to me just how wrong the Sadducees were. I beheld the Glory of Heaven as the angels were more numerous and magnificent than mere words can justify. While I was in awe of the sheer number of angels it became quickly apparent the angels were in awe of Jesus Christ, the Lamb of God. With power and splendor, they sang before their creator I chronicled this experience down I wrote in the book of Revelation, 'Then I looked and heard the voice of many angels, numbering thousands upon thousands, and ten thousand times ten thousand. They encircled the throne and the living creatures and the elders. In a loud voice they sang: 'Worthy is the Lamb, who was slain, to receive power and wealth and wisdom and strength and honor and glory and praise!'" (Revelation 5:11-12).

Summarizing the three different views John stated, "For the Pharisees, their confidence was in their own works. For the Sadducees their worth was found entirely in their temporary wealth and power. For the Essenes, their peace was found in separation from the rest of society. As the trek for Andrew and I was coming to end, we were approaching John the Baptist, a man whose message implored others not to place their confidence in their own works, wealth, or isolation.

Instead, John the Baptist was calling for everyone to,

"Repent, for the Kingdom of God is near" (Matthew 3:1-2).

Chapter 2 Footnotes

[1] After the arrest of Jesus, we read in John 18:15- "Simon Peter and another disciple were following Jesus. Because this disciple was known to the high priest, he went with Jesus to the high priest's courtyard." Here the adjective that is used for "was known" is gnóstos. (biblehub) This means, "known, an acquaintance." This depiction isn't one where Caiaphas would "have heard of John", but they knew each other. John knew Caiaphas and Caiaphas knew John. According to Franciscan legend it states that John's family provided fish to the high priest's family [C] John was young but old enough to carry out the duty assigned to him. Reasoning behind why Andrew was with him takes some logic and rational. John and Andrew were the two disciples of Jesus who were first disciples of John. Considering the location where John the Baptist was, east of the Jordan River and not that far North of the Dead Sea, it makes sense that they first saw him after coming from Jerusalem. If they made a trip around Passover, they would have been with there entire family. The Zebedee family business would have made multiple transaction in Jerusalem throughout the year and since at times Peter and Andrew appeared to work together with Zebedee's business, it is not farfetched to think that Andrew accompanied John to complete a business transaction in Jerusalem, heard about John the Baptist and decided to further investigate what was taking place.

[2] The title Governor was initially called prefects because they had a military role. This title was later changed to procurator which was done to stress their role as being financially responsible for the region they were given the responsibility to govern. [F]

[3] Chronologically these events were taking place, around the time when Andrew and John would have both been disciples of John the Baptist and Pontius Pilate would have been the governor of Judea, probably in his second year. John Calvin [G] quotes from Josephus in his commentary describing the events in Luke 3 to show how the Governor appointed by Rome had the authority over the appointing of a high priest and could change who high priest was whenever they desired. Josephus stated of Pilate's predecessor Valerius Gratus "This man (Valerius Gratus) deprived Ananus of the high priesthood, and appointed Ishmael, the son of Phabi, to be high priest. He also deprived him in a little time, and

ordained Eleazar, the son of Ananus, who had been high priest before, to be high priest: which office, when he had held for a year, Gratus deprived him of it, and gave the high priesthood to Simon, the son of Camithus; and, when he had possessed that dignity no longer than a year, Joseph Caiaphas was made his successor. When Gratus had done those things, he went back to Rome, after he had tarried in Judea eleven years, when Pontius Pilate came as his successor." — [1]

[4] Caiaphas was high priest from 18-36 A.D. [L]

[5] There is no mention of how Andrew and John first heard about John the Baptist or what caused them to become his disciples. The conversation between Caiaphas and Annas, overheard by Andrew and John was purely speculative. Scripture does inform us religious leaders of Jerusalem heard about the ministry of John the Baptist and sent priests and Levities to investigate (John 1:19). Events surrounding Andrew and John becoming disciples of John the Baptist are unknown. We do know their businesses worked together, Zebedee had business with the high priest's family in Jerusalem, and Andrew and John became disciples of John the Baptist.

[6] The Galileans described as passionate, impulsive, and caring more for honor than money is found in the Talmud. Differences between the mindset of Judeans and Galileans are the Judeans, where Jerusalem and the Temple was located, was run by Rabbinism and Galilee was not. This naturally allowed for the Galileans to have a greater sense of freedom and thought in action than the Judeans. Additionally, Josephus summarized the Galileans by saying that they "had always resisted any hostile invasion and were from infancy inured to war" and also stated that, "the most famous feature of the Galileans was their independence." [O] This independent mindset was evident based on the actions of Peter, Andrew, James, John and the other Galilean disciples who went against what would be considered the norm in many circles of thought by leaving behind something that is established to follow Jesus who was bringing into fruition a new teaching and ultimately a new covenant with God and man. The Apostles Andrew and John following a man who was bringing about a radical new teaching not once, but twice by being followers of John the Baptist, the forerunner of the Messiah, and ultimately the Messiah, Jesus Christ. In fact, of the twelve disciples the only who was not from Galilee and who was from Judah was Judas Iscariot. Iscariot is broken down to show that *ish* means "man" and Kerioth is a town in the South of Judah so Iscariot literally means, "man of Kerioth." [P] So the only one of the twelve not from Galilee was the betrayer.

[7] We do not know the exact location of Bethany or *Bethabara* as it is also referred to as. [T] Since the Apostle John describes its location as "beyond the Jordan", he is distinguishing from the more famous Bethany which is

only about two miles from Jerusalem. This Bethany would be an obscure village on the eastern side of the Jordan River.

[8] As was mentioned earlier Eusebius, the 4th century Christian historian the Apostle John was alive, in Asia (modern day Turkey) "until the times of Trajan." [Y] Trajan became emperor of Rome in AD 98. During the Jewish revolt against Rome which lasted from AD 66-74 the key event was the destruction of the Temple in AD 70. [Z] Of the Pharisees, Sadducees, and Essenes, only the Pharisees would last after the devastation of the Jewish Revolt. Rabbinic Judaism concentrated on the study of the Torah rather than the Temple which ceased to exist after its destruction. [AA]

[9] "holy ones" is another term given to angels [KK]

[10] Of the 66 books in the Bible, 34 of these books refer to angels by using the term angel and this term is used more than 300 times in the Bible. [LL]

Chapter 3

The Wilderness Prophet

Matthew 3:1-12; Mark 1:2-8; Luke 3:2-15

As John continued to explain the experiences of Andrew and himself, the elderly apostle's voice perked up as he described the anticipation two must have felt mere moments before witnessing the man who was the forerunner to the Messiah. "Finally, the moment was at hand. Seeing a gathering of people up ahead, hearing the commotion, mystery and intrigue of the situation was overwhelming. We wondered if we would quickly be able to decipher what sect or group of people John the Baptist belonged too. Was he a Pharisee? Sadducee? Essene? Or maybe even a Zealot? We were amazed to discover that John the Baptist was none of those, instead belonging to an entirely different group of people, while being entirely unique for this day. John the Baptist was one of a group of people that, up to this point, only existed in the past history of the Jewish culture. For the first time in four and half centuries, for the first time since Malachi spoke to the people of Judea following the exile, the Hebrew people had a prophet of God, and his name was John the Baptist."

Maneuvering our way through the crowd and finally caught a glimpse of this religious reformer whose attire was radically different a priestly robe. Upon further analysis it became apparent that John the Baptist wasn't meant to blend in rather he was being used by God to transform. Before John the Baptist arrived on the scene a common saying among the Hebrew people, "There was no voice, nor any that answered" [A] showing the people recognized they had no prophet during their day. It had been four and a half centuries since the Hebrew people had a prophet, but they had one now. The last prophetic word of Malachi was the promise of someone who would resemble another prophet, the prophet Elijah. Malachi wrote, "See, I will send you the prophet Elijah before that great and dreadful day of the LORD comes. He will turn the hearts of the fathers to their children, and the hearts of the children to their fathers; or else I will come and strike the land with a curse" (Malachi 4:5-6 NIV).

"Why was this day called, 'the great and dreadful day of the LORD?' This would seem to be a contradictory statement"[1] reasoned Papias.

"My son, when the King emerges to claim His Kingdom, this is a great event for those who are faithful and loyal to the King but a terrible day for those who are traitorous to His rule. John the Baptist was the forerunner for King Jesus, a Kingdom unique to the history of the world, an eternal kingdom centered and founded on the righteousness of God. This kingdom does not demand its citizens prove worthy through the might of conquest but rather through the humility of confession. John the Baptist was now playing the role of prophet proclaiming the coming of a King who even King David recognized was superior to him in power and authority. God raised up John the Baptist so that King Jesus would have a forerunner to prepare a way for those that will be a part of His Kingdom. This forerunner does not begin by training the subjects for war but rather preparing their hearts to be repentant."

"While listening, I felt a sense of urgency to make my way to speak to John the Baptist. Would he remember my family? Did he know who I was? Occasionally I would hear my parents bring him up as well as his father Zacharias and mother Elizabeth but none of us foresaw John having this kind of impact."

"While making our way to the front, the prophet elaborated on his message, 'This is the fulfillment of that which we have hoped for, which we have longed for. You have studied the Torah and read the Books of Moses. I tell you God's commands as revealed to Moses was more than to sanctify

His people and show they are separate from all the nations in the world, but rather the fulfillment of a greater promise, the promise of the Kingdom of God.'"

"'How can this be true' said the voice of a dissenter from the crowd. 'You claim your message is of the LORD yet here we being ruled by those are not our brethren, paying taxes for the kingdom of a pagan ruler, and soldiers occupy this land not armed to fight for the nation of Israel but ready to oppress the people of this so called, 'promised land.' Yet you claim to have a message from God.' After hearing a voice of dissension the crowd began to murmur among themselves. Briefly, it felt like doubt was seeping into some of their minds as they began to wonder if the curiosity that caused them to travel a considerable distance was only to hear nothing more than a fanatic blurting out false hope. With all eyes now solely focused on the wilderness preacher, he gave a piercing glare at the man who spoke out in opposition before walking towards him with a pace that seemed to quicken until he stood directly in front of the man. Seeds of doubt were now planted into the minds of the crowd, and the baptizer was prepared to answer

"John the Baptists demeanor and tenacity caused a clamoring crown to become silent. 'By what authority do you speak? Are you able to use Scripture to oppose what I have been

preaching? Have you been sent by God to quiet my voice?'
John the Baptist demanded from the man questioning the
legitimacy of the prophet. All the heads of the people in the
crowd turned in unison to see how the dissenter would
respond. Silence! Silence from the man who had rebuked the
wilderness preacher, and besides a collective gasp the crowd
was silent as well. Since the skeptic had nothing to say John
continued, 'does a man seek power and fame by living in
isolation in the barren wilderness? I have no worldly
possessions so explain to me, what is my motivation for
being here? Yet you have the audacity to question my
motives yet cast a blind eye when the Temple is used by the
religious elites to rapidly increase their wealth. Are you
blinded to your own hypocrisy? My message is of
righteousness and your rejection reveals the condition of your
heart, yet one more time I implore you, repent for the
Kingdom of Heaven is near.'
As the echo of John's words dissipated the only sound that
could be heard was the noise of the faint wind in the
background. Too proud to recant his words and accept John's
message of repentance and feeling embarrassed after being
thoroughly dominated in this exchange the man left publicly
opposed the message no more."

Briefly stopping to gather his thoughts, John transitioned from fiery defense to passionate plea for everyone there to embrace the validity of his message. "I ask you all; can God go against His Word? If you have read the books of Moses our current state under the authority of Rome should come as a surprise to no one for God is being true to what He has said. Shortly before his death Moses' words from the LORD were both a command and a warning. In the third and final discourse of Deuteronomy Moses stated, "But if you will not obey the LORD your God or be careful to do all His commandments and his statues that I command you today, then all these curses shall come upon you and overtake you." (Deuteronomy 28:15 ESV). Truly our LORD is 'slow to anger and abounding in love' (Exodus 34:6, Numbers 14:18, Psalm 86:15, Psalm 103:8) but to reject the command of God is to choose instead to accept His judgment. Even now, God is ready to show His mercy, even now, the LORD is ready to offer forgiveness, even now, YHWH is providing a path of salvation. Our Sovereign LORD still offers rest and salvation to His People. Repent, for the Kingdom of heaven[2] is near'" (Matthew 3:2).

Further explaining to his pupils the culture dynamics of that day, the Apostle John continued, "Devout Jews of this day had a difficult time accepting not only that they were governed by a foreign ruler, but their rulers were pagans and idolatrous. [B] Difficult for many to rationalize yet this was consistent with the Word of God and the warning given in Deuteronomy. Many focused on their present reality. John the Baptist proclaimed an upcoming certainty, the Kingdom of God was near. [C]

While John preached Andrew whispered to me, 'Look at what he is wearing.'

'What is it?' I responded.

'I think its camel hair and a leather belt (Mark 1:6), just like Elijah' Andrew answered.

 This was a great sign about the role that John the Baptist was set apart by God to fulfill. By the time this wilderness prophet started preaching and baptizing in the Jordan Valley it would have been about nine centuries since the ministry of Elijah started. The children of Israel never had a prophet like Elijah before him or since. That is, until, John the Baptist arrived on the scene.[3] The attire of John the Baptist is more than just relevant in its symbolic connection with Elijah, a prophet of ages past, but also significant for the day in which he prophesied. John the Baptist was not striving to be viewed as elegant teacher whose domain would be found in a synagogue in Judea or Galilee. This description does not fit him and therefore the attire of a teacher of the law wouldn't be apt for him to wear. He was a man of the wilderness. His 'classroom' was the banks of the Jordan River. His lodging was the rough residence of the mountains. [E] Wild honey and locusts were available for consumption, so this became the appropriate nourishment for the wilderness prophet. Accordingly, his appearance and his diet had to match his habitat. His appearance was a connection to Elijah nine centuries earlier as well as a profound statement of the modern day in which he preached and prophesied."

"Apostle, why the focus on Elijah?" questioned Polycarp.

"I was thinking the same thing", chimed in Papias before continuing, "Not to minimize Elijah, he was one of the most unique and influential individuals in the Scriptures, but if his ministry was almost nine centuries earlier why not just focus on John the Baptist since God was doing a new work?"

"Teknion" (little/dear children), "few things are more memorable and profound than last words. Throughout Scripture we have seen that last words are often times a source of great hope. Think of the patriarch Joseph and his last recorded words in the book of Genesis, 'And Joseph took an oath of the children of Israel, saying, 'God will surely visit you, and ye shall carry up my bones from hence'' (Genesis 50:25 KJV). Altogether the children of Israel were in Egypt 430 years (Exodus 12:40). During the period of slavery and

oppression, how many do you think would have held on to the prophetic words of Joseph that God would come to them? We can say for certain that this was a source of hope as well as obedience, for when the children of Israel left Egypt, Moses made sure that they honored the oath that was given to Joseph and they took his bones with them. Now, once again the Hebrew people found themselves under foreign rule. Approximately 430 years before the birth of John the Baptist and Jesus, the last prophetic words recorded by the last prophet until this time said, 'See, I will send you the prophet Elijah before that great and dreadful day of the LORD comes. He will turn the hearts of the fathers to their children, and the hearts of the children to their fathers; or else I will come and strike the land with a curse'(Malachi 4:5-6-NIV). This was a promise and a warning, and these words are what the children of Israel held onto for over 450 years by the time the prophetic ministry of John the Baptist began. Our dear brother in the LORD Luke recorded in his Gospel the words the angel sent by God had spoken to Zechariah regards to his son John, 'And he will go before the LORD, in the spirit and power of Elijah, to turn their hearts of the fathers to the children and the disobedient to the wisdom of the righteous-to make ready a people prepared for the LORD' (Luke 1:17). My sons, read the Scriptures of the Old Testament, you will find that never was there a preacher or prophet like Elijah. When I was in my youth and surrounded by young and old to hear John the Baptist preach, we all were likeminded in our analysis, never had we heard anyone speak like John the Baptist. Truly he had come in the spirit and power of Elijah, anointed for this unique calling. He was a prophet whose ministry was a fulfillment of prophecy."

"Now John the Baptist and Elijah are not literally the same person. God did not send Elijah down from heaven to be the messenger who would proclaim the coming of the Messiah. However, John the Baptist did come in the spirit and power of Elijah (Luke 1:17). When the ministry of John the Baptist began, the prophecy pertaining to Elijah was fulfilled, and this meant the Messiah would soon be on the scene. The authentic message of the wilderness prophet challenged all in attendance to respond to the call, "you who consider yourselves religious, recognize genuine repentance must be our reaction to sin." [H] The prophet Isaiah wrote, "Let the wicked forsake his way, and the unrighteous man his thoughts; Let him return to the LORD, and He will have mercy on him; and to our God, for He will abundantly pardon" (Isaiah 55:7 KJV).

From the crowd approached a man with genuine sincerity, falling to his knees in humble recognition that the ministry of John the Baptist was of the LORD.[4] "Who are you? Are you the Christ?" he asked. With genuine warms John smiled at the man who asked the question that was on many minds of those in attendance.

John the Baptist looked at the crowd and loudly proclaimed, "A voice of one calling in the desert, 'Prepare the way for the LORD, make straight paths for him. Every valley shall be filled in, every mountain and hill made low. The crooked roads shall become straight, the rough ways smooth. And all mankind will see God's salvation"[5] (Luke 3:4-6 NIV).

"As the powerful voice of the prophet echoed throughout the Jordan Valley [1] it didn't take long before representatives of the religious establishment approached. John peered past the crowd and give an intense glare at a faction of individuals who were making their way towards him. As the sea of people parted to give a clear aisle for these distinguished men and they were in clearer view, I instantaneously recognized them."

"Pharisees and Sadducees from Jerusalem" Andrew stated factually.

"Yes I know", I answered, "They must have been sent by Annas and Caiaphas." Curiosity and intrigue brought me to the Jordan Valley but I didn't want to jeopardize my father's good standing with the men of influence in which his business benefitted greatly.

As they stood there together one of the Sadducees stepped forward from amongst the others and boldly questioned, "What is this gathering of people assembled along the Jordan River?" stated the man with outstretched arms as he turns to face the crowd of people while John the Baptist glared at the man with earnest focus.

"Are you like Moses bringing YHWH's chosen people back into the wilderness? Shall we next expect manna from heaven? Although the way that you are dressed it would appear that you are Elijah. Shall I look for the prophets of Baal? Is there a sacrifice set up that will be consumed by fire from heaven?"

Rather than go on the defensive, the wilderness preacher responded in a fervent retaliation, "You brood of vipers!" John the Baptist boldly proclaimed with thunderous resolve using, imagery to which he was well accustomed. "Who warned you to flee from the coming wrath?" (Matthew 3:7; Luke 3:7). This temporarily silenced the entire delegation for never had they been spoken to in this manner before. Most of the Jewish people would show respect for the position of authority they held, but titles of man never caused admiration on the part of prophets of the Old Testament, and John the Baptist was cut from the same mold. "Does God find your titles, your riches, your wealth, your earthly power to be worthy of esteem? Will being given titles from Rome allow for you to be righteous in the eyes of God?" "Bear fruit in keeping with repentance" (Luke 3:8a)[6]

Another man from amongst the group, this time a Pharisee, stepped forward to offer justification on their behalf. "We are children of Abraham, his direct descendants. If the father to our people was righteous in the eyes of God without the necessity to be immersed in the Jordan River, then what is the necessity of this display? Gentiles need to take part in ritual cleansing in order to worship YHWH, but as descendants of Abraham and followers of the law our righteousness is secured."

Immediately after the last word left the lips of this notable religious leader, John the Baptist fired back his reply. "Why was Abraham declared righteous? Because of his lineage? Because of his titles and position? Abraham lived in tents and was a stranger and foreigner in the land that we today call home (Hebrews 11:9). Yet your righteousness comes because you are part of his lineage? No, we read that, "Abram believed the LORD, and He credited it to him as righteousness" (Genesis 15:6). "How then can you claim to righteous because of Abraham, yet you are inwardly corrupt? Your righteousness is found only on the outside; inwardly you need to be made pure. [K] God raised up a people who were slaves and called them His own. They were descendants of Abraham, were they not? What was their response? They cried out to the LORD for help and God heard their cry and groaning, and He delivered them. You say, "We are descendants of Abraham." As God revealed He can make the dry bones become flesh (Ezekiel 37),

This tense standoff continued to escalate when another man from the group with his teeth grit and fists clenched stepped forward and said, "We are children of Abraham," emphasizing their genealogy as their means of justification. "Bear fruit in keeping with repentance. And do not begin to say to yourselves, 'We have Abraham as our father.' For I tell you, God is able to, from these stones to raise up children for Abraham.' (Luke 3:8 ESV). Once again, I urge you, repent, for the Kingdom of Heaven is near. One last dissenting voice then answered, "Or, what, judgment?" "Repent?" The voice of the Pharisee screamed. "Repent?" the man said even louder the second time. "Then what, judgment?" The man yelled in a manner of defiance.

"The ax is already at the root of the tree" John the Baptist responded, refusing to be shaken. Yet his face did not show anger of one being rejected but rather compassion to those rejecting the message of which he was sent to deliver. "You are Pharisees and Sadducees that stand before me today. One (Pharisees) emphasizes the law and the support of the people. The other (Sadducees) emphasizes titles given by Rome and wealth. You both agree on so little, yet here you are, unified in opposition to the work of the LORD and the fulfillment of the law and the prophets. You are so steeped in tradition that you are losing sight of fulfillment of Scriptures. "Cast away from you all the transgressions you have committed and make yourselves a new heart and a new spirit! Why will you die, O house of Israel?" (Ezekiel 18:31 ESV). You claim to be descendants of Abraham. Don't you see how this goes deeper than genealogy? We are the people for whom God made His Covenant. Yet you do not walk with God as Abraham walked with God, or talk to God as Moses talked with God. You walked through a wilderness to hear a message that offers life, but if you reject this message, reject the need to judge yourselves and see that you need to repent your sins to God, you will be judged by God. I implore you, Repent for the Kingdom of Heaven is near!

"We have heard enough", the lead Sadducee boldly stated. He turned his back towards John the Baptist and began the path back towards Jerusalem. The rest of the delegation followed suit. That is except for one man, who stood there looking at John the Baptist.

"Repent" the prophet stated again, this time speaking to an audience of one. It was apparent he desired to come forward, his heart felt compelled to live up to the Covenant established between God and His chosen people.

"Simon", a voice yelled in an authoritative manner, "we are going back to Jerusalem."

"Repent", John the Baptist stated once more. Simon the Pharisee was in the midst of a battle. The tradition from which he was reared verses the conviction of the message of John the Baptist. There was a pause before Simon slowly turned around and joined the group walking back to report all that they had seen. In this instance, pressure trumped conviction.[7]

According to the message preached by John the Baptist, repentance and baptism are more important than an individual's ancestry and whether or not they were circumcised. [L] John immediately transitioned into the offer to any who would accept the invitation to be baptized.[8]

"I am going", stated Andrew walking towards the banks of the Jordan River. Andrew may have been viewed at times as impulsive, but I prefer to view him as passionately following his convictions which he repeatedly had done and this time was no exception. John the Baptist made his way into the River to baptize those who were accepting of his message of repentance, and be filled with hope over the soon to be arrival of the Messiah.

"So am I", I said to Andrew as I made my way in line awaiting my turn.

Before the baptisms were about to take place, John the Baptist addressed the crowd of gatherers one final time, "As Moses wrote down the Law of Purification, before Eleazar the priest would be considered clean, he was to sacrifice a red heifer and then sprinkle the blood of the heifer seven times in front of the Tabernacle. Before the priest was considered clean, first he was to wash his clothes in water and then bathe in water (Numbers 19:1-10). This was not just an act of symbolism but also an act of obedience. One in which the priest was to also adhere to before coming before God in a manner the LORD deemed as worthy. Come now and be baptized and embrace this washing as a sign for what is yet to take place." M

While in line we watched John repeatedly utter the phrase, "I baptize you with water unto repentance" (Matthew 3:11). Andrew was in front of me trudging through the water until it was waist high to meet the baptizer in the Jordan River. "Are you here to make a public declaration that you are ready to be counted among God's people?" asked John the Baptist.

Andrew answered in affirmation, and after he confessed his sins, [9] John the Baptist declared to Andrew and all who were in attendance, "I baptize you with water unto repentance."

As I watched my close friend brought out of the water, a look of exhilaration came across his face. John the Baptist smiled, put his arm around Andrew and asked him, "Where are you from?"

Andrew answered, "I am a fisherman with my brother Simon from Capernaum. I travelled here with your relative."

Seemingly caught off guard John asked "My relative?"

Andrew simply nodded his head and then pointed over towards me, and as the man with a prophetic message from God tried to put the puzzle together of who I was, it was apparent the moment when he recognized me. His face changed, and he smiled and said, "The younger son of Zebedee and Salome am I correct?"

I didn't know what to say, I never spoke to a prophet before so I just smiled and nodded my head.

"How could I forget my namesake," said John the Baptist, jokingly referring to the fact that we share the same name. "I see the resemblance now. It has been so long since I have seen you; you were but a young child. Do you remember me?" he asked.

Honestly, I was so young when I met John and his parents Zacharias and Elizabeth. I remembered the trip but was unable to recall anything about our actual meeting. Embarrassed, I didn't want to admit that I couldn't remember meeting him, but I also thought that, for the first time in over four centuries, God had sent a prophet to His people, and it wouldn't be a good idea to lie during our first conversation. "I heard a lot about you and your parents but I am sorry to say I don't remember meeting you."

"I wouldn't expect you to" John the Baptist said reassuringly. "Now, far more important than our inadvertent mini-family reunion that has taken place, are you here to make a public declaration that you are ready to be counted among God's people?"

"Yes, yes I am" I stated with assurance and confidence. After confessing my sins John the Baptist then said, "I baptize you with water unto repentance."

This event lasted but a moment yet it's significance was life altering. This reformer upset the social balance that had been established by speaking a message that resonated with crowds of people from Judea and Galilee unlike any man in centuries before him, and now I was his disciple. As a fisherman, I was used to being in the water, but there I was, a saturated teenager, looking at a smiling prophet, and I blurted out, "I will follow you anywhere."

John the Baptist responded, "I have no doubt you would young Galilean. However, God's ultimate plan is not that you follow me for long. For there is one who is coming after me who is far greater than I; in fact, as I will tell others, His sandal strap I am unworthy to loose.[10] My desire for you is that you follow Him. Wait for me, and when I am finished preaching and baptizing for the day, we will talk more before you head back to Galilee."

As I walked out of the water, over seven decades earlier, I didn't fully understand the significance of the event. Flowing into the Dead Sea, the Jordan River was commonly referred to as "the river of death." [O] Yet, being baptized that day, I was given a new purpose, and a hope that one who was still to come would provide an even greater deliverance. [P] While I didn't know all that God had in store, I was excited to find out and I rejoiced, because the "Kingdom of Heaven was near."

Early Life of John the Baptist
Luke 1:5-25; 57-66

After joining Andrew on the banks of the Jordan, we listened to a few more hours of preaching and baptisms before John the Baptist, prophet, wilderness preacher, and forerunner to Christ joined us to continue our brief dialogue.

"Well, let me start from the beginning. I know that parents all the time look at their newborn child and confess that they must be a miracle. Now, in my case, people were looking not at me but at my parents and saying this was a miracle, for they were past the age when they should be able to have children. My parents were righteous in the eyes of God (Luke 1:6), faithful servants and humble in nature. My father Zacharias had not only the genealogy, but also the heart to serve as a priest.

There were about 20,000 priests during this era, ^Q so it would be difficult for one to distinguish himself among his peers, but this role was never the goal of my father. Approximately half of the priests at this time had a permanent residence in the city of Jerusalem and around 25 percent of the priests lived in the affluent city of Jericho, known as the "City of Palms." ^R My parents were in the other 25 percent, choosing to live a simplistic lifestyle in poverty in the hill country of Judea (Luke 1:39). Despite their humble living and faithful service, both my parents found difficulties, not so much in their lack of material possessions, but rather in their inability to have children.

King David, about 1,000 years earlier, divided the priesthood into 24 divisions (I Chronicles 24:1-19). My father was of the division of Abijah (Luke 1:5). During Passover and Pentecost, all of the priests were called into service. During the rest of the year each division of the priesthood would serve on a one-week rotation twice a year, so altogether my father would be serving in Jerusalem for four weeks out of every year. During their week of service, the priests would cast lots to see who would enter into the Holy Place to burn incense each morning and each evening (Exodus 30:7). When the lots fell in favor of my father, he subsequently viewed this as the pinnacle of his act of service as a priest. With such a large number of priests, not everyone was given the honor of burning the incense during their priestly ministry. This was truly a once in a lifetime event, for no priest was permitted to serve in this manner twice. [5] Gathered worshipers were honoring God outside and my father braced himself when walking into the Holy Place. While only priests were allowed in the Holy Place, my father would be put in even more selective company, standing in the presence of the angel Gabriel. Fear and terror gripped my father while standing in the presence of this celestial being. Immediately the powerful presence of Gabriel spoke reassuring words to my father saying, "Do not be afraid" (Luke 1:13).

If there was ever a time my father needed assurance it was at that moment. Gabriel shared that my parent's prayers were answered and their shame and disgrace for being childless was coming to an end. My mother would give birth to a child. Gabriel explained that I was to be a Nazarene. Scripture made clear that those who would take the vow of a Nazirite would follow these rules until the vow was completed. For the priest, they were not to drink any wine or intoxicating drink while in the tabernacle (Leviticus 10:9). Additionally no grape juice, grapes and raisins until the duration of the vow was completed (Numbers 6:3-4). I would not serve as a priest in the Temple like my father before me; prior to even being born, I was dedicated to God for my entire life. [T] I was to be filled with the Holy Spirit at all times rather than being filled with wine at any time (Luke 1:15). While I was in my mother, the Holy Spirit was within me. My parents made the conscientious decision to have my mother go into seclusion for five months of her pregnancy. My father struggled initially accepting the prophetic message of Gabriel that my mother would conceive a child after spending what would be considered her child bearing years completely barren. As a result, he was stricken with the inability to speak and would remain that way until his written declaration that my name was John when I was eight days old and brought to be circumcised. If my father were still here, I don't believe that the irony would be lost on him that my prophet ministry was centered on having and being "the voice of one calling in the desert." The name John (*Johanan*) means, "gift of God." [U] God's gift to my mother took away her disgrace (Luke 1:25) and revealed my parents had found favor with the LORD.

As the years passed, and I grew in greater understanding of the things of the LORD, I became grieved by how society was functioning. Being filled by the Holy Spirit means you grieve the same things that grieve God. Solitude with God became more appealing than associating with society. So I was led by the Spirit to a place where my only communion would be with God. I settled in the Judean Wilderness, West of the Dead Sea, and lived of abstinence. [V] This became a time of personal preparation for my unique ministry; to prepare the way for the Messiah. I remained in the wilderness until the LORD revealed it was time to go to the banks of the

Jordan River. Our ancestors wandered in the wilderness for 40 years until YHWH delivered them into the land that He had promised to them. We shall soon see a Revelation that exceeds the gift of the Promised Land to the children of Israel and that is the promised Messiah.

"When will that be", I remember asking the wilderness prophet.

"Soon", answered John the Baptist with a smile. "Now go tell your families what you have seen, what you have experienced, and what you have done as an act of repentance and obedience. Tell them that I am a messenger preparing the way of the LORD (Malachi 3:1)." With that Andrew and I headed back to Galilee eager to share our experiences. John the Baptist had a radical message; he was preparing the way for the Messiah.

First Year of Ministry for Jesus
John 1:19-4:54

As Andrew and I discussed our excitement over the events that had just transpired, it dawned on us that after we settled back into Galilee we would be hard-pressed to get as excited about fishing.

"It's tough to go back to how things were before," I told Andrew during our walk back to Galilee.

"Well we are going back", Andrew answered, "but I don't think that things will be the same as they were before. This trip changes everything," he concluded.

After we reached Galilee, Andrew headed towards Capernaum and I went to my parent's home in Bethsaida. "I will see you tomorrow by the boats," he said as we were heading our separate ways.

"I thought our trip changed everything" I amusingly replied. Andrew stopped, turned to look at me and said, "It does change everything, for tomorrow when we are fishing, our topic of conversation will rarely be about fish."

After arriving home, my mother was relieved that I was alright after being gone for longer than expected. My father, ever the businessman and eager to get me back on the fishing boats, inquired as to why the delay.

"Well, I sort of ran into a family member" I answered.

"Who?" they asked surprisingly.

"I heard the preaching of John, the son of Zacharias and Elizabeth."

"What?" they answered in a shocked reply.

"We haven't seen him in years", stated my father, "he was such a mystery."

"Always has been a mystery", reiterated my mother. "When I was but a girl, my older sister Mary visited Elizabeth at her home in the hill country of Judea (Luke 1:36; 39). Despite her advanced age, we received news that Elizabeth was miraculously pregnant for the first time. Shortly thereafter, I found out my older sister Mary was already pregnant with your cousin Jesus despite being so young and not properly married. This is truly shocking that you met up with John. Where has he been the last several years? After the death of his parents we haven't heard anything about him.[11] Then I shared that John had been in the Judean Wilderness, waiting for God to reveal His prophetic ministry. W

I proceeded to share with my parents all that Andrew and I heard and witnessed. "So is he the Messiah?" my brother James scoffed, as he was surprisingly quiet up to this point. "No", I answered, "he claims to be the forerunner for the one through whom the LORD will do an even greater work." "What does this mean for you?" my father asked. "Well, I am a disciple of John the Baptist now, so Andrew and I will be going back, and James, we would like for you to come with us." James shook his head in a disgusted manner, "We have a business to run. Yet you think it's wiser to listen to a man who spent years in solitude in the wilderness?" Why can't God speak to me when I am actually being productive and fishing in the Sea of Galilee?" With that James revealed he had no interest in being a follower of anyone. That would change upon being given the invitation to be a disciple of Jesus but for now he chose to pursue fishing over a prophet of God.[12]

Modern Day Application-Wilderness Experience

One of the recurring themes throughout Scripture is "the wilderness experience" in which God uses challenging times of isolation to profoundly shape the lives of His followers. Abraham obeyed God and travelled 600 miles of open space or wilderness [X] road from Haran to Canaan (Genesis 12:4-9). Before being sold to the Ishmaelites and taken into Egypt, the Patriarch Joseph was tossed into a cistern while in the wilderness (Genesis 37:22).[13] When YHWH spoke to Moses by the burning bush at Horeb, the mountain of God, Moses was in the wilderness (Exodus 3:1-6). Elijah the prophet was fleeing from Queen Jezebel, left Beersheba and went out into the wilderness (I Kings 19:4). God sent an angel to speak to Elijah and gave him food for his journey to Horeb, the same mountain that God spoke to the prophet Moses about 6 centuries earlier (I Kings 19:7-18). You also probably won't find this surprising, but Horeb was in the wilderness. God did not intend for "the wilderness" to destroy these individuals but rather lead them to unprecedented spiritual growth in their own lives.

Odds are, most of us will not find ourselves in an extended stay in a literal wilderness, and, symbolically, the "wilderness experience" should not be viewed as only taking place in a literal wilderness. God uses circumstances to stretch and grow us in order that we might recognize our dependency on Him and, with gracious hearts, embrace being benefactors of His grace. When difficulties arise such as being laid off from a job, health problems, foreclosure of a home, loss of a loved one, relational problems, struggles and with depression, all of these and more are examples of what could have been your own personal "wilderness experience." Anytime a believer goes through a "wilderness experience," it does not occur so the individual experiences their own strength and abilities. Rather it occurs that the individual might experience God.

For over two centuries many Americans have found inspiration from the United States battle for independence in the Revolutionary War. Against all odds, this band of Patriots refused to give up and, with the help of France, defeated the most powerful empire in the world at that time. For me personally, the most iconic image of the war didn't occur after a major victory like defeating General Lord Cornwallis at Yorktown, or even the depiction of George Washington crossing the Delaware. The greatest image of strength for the father of a new nation was at his greatest moment of weakness: when Washington, alone with nobody but his horse, head down and knee bent during the frigid winter at Valley Forge, prays to God, for he has no place else to turn. At this time, due to various differences of opinions, Washington's relationship with Congress was as glum as the frigid temperature during the winter of 1777-1778. [Y] Supplies low, morale lower, and General Horatio Gates politicking to replace Washington as lead General, [Z] make no mistake, for George Washington this was a "wilderness experience." When Washington's soldiers were looking to him for guidance and provision, the army was sparse on blankets, clothes, shoes, and food. Subsequently, it was described that his men, while walking barefoot, were leaving behind blood stained tracks in the snow. Arguably, there is no more esteemed leader in the history of the United States than George Washington, but I would be hard pressed to imagine the feeling of inadequacy was prevalent at this time. The severe hardship of this horrid winter was as demoralizing as any military defeat. This leads to the lasting image of Washington, no soldiers around him, only his white horse beside him, bended knee in the snow, faced downward, and seeking the aid of his all-sufficient God to meet the overwhelming circumstances he was facing. During the winter of 1777-1778 Washington sought the LORD for strength to see him through this challenging season. When describing the winter at Valley Forge, Washington stated, "While we are zealously performing the duties of good Citizens and soldiers, we certainly ought not to be inattentive to the higher duties of Religion. To the distinguished Character of Patriot, it should be our highest Glory to add the more distinguished Character of Christian." AA

Your "wilderness experience" most likely will not take place during a frigid winter at Valley Forge like George Washington, or the intense heat and isolation of the Judean Wilderness like John the Baptist, but I firmly believe that every Christian symbolically will go through wilderness experiences during their walk with the LORD. Often, these experiences make you feel isolated, but they are actually meant to draw you closer to God. Rest assured you're in good company when you go through challenging times. Abraham, Jacob, Joseph, Moses, David, and John the Baptist are just a few of the Scriptural examples. Even Jesus went through a "wilderness experience" and as a result He is not unable to "sympathize with our weaknesses" (Hebrews 4:15). Your wilderness experience is not meant to destroy you; it's meant to transform you. So when you are going through a "wilderness" be encouraged and draw closer to the LORD allowing God to do a mighty work in your life.

Chapter 3 Footnotes

[1] In Malachi 4:5 the coming of the prophesied Elijah is described as "great and dreadful." The reason for the varied consequences centers on the response of the people. To simplify, John the Baptist was calling for people to repent. For those who were obedient the day of the LORD was great. For those who were disobedient the day of the LORD was dreadful. The Hebrew transliteration for the word "dreadful" used in Malachi 4:5 is *yare* which literally means "affright" (biblehub.com) This is the same Hebrew word used in Genesis 3:10 when Adam speaks to God after his sin was exposed and Adam described himself as "afraid." Genesis 3:10- "He answered, 'I heard you in the garden, and I was afraid because I was naked; so I hid." Interesting parallel that near the beginning of the Old Testament in Genesis 3 we see the consequences for the sin of man after the LORD comes. Then the Old Testament ends by giving a warning for the consequences to those who fail to confess their sins. In the 23rd book of the New Testament, the Apostle John will emphasize the importance of confessing your sin to God when he writes I John 1:9- "If we confess our sins, He is faithful and just to forgive us our sins and cleanse us from all unrighteousness" (KJV). This is a lesson that the Apostle John would have learned as a disciple of both John the Baptist and Jesus, as well as the inspiration of the Holy Spirit.

[2] The term "Kingdom of heaven" is only found in the Gospel of Matthew (Matthew 3:2; 13:44) but the term "Kingdom of God is found in all four Gospels [D] (Matthew 6:33, Mark 1:15; 4:11, 26, 30, 15:43, Luke 18:29, John 3:3, 5)

[3] Most of the prophetic ministry of Elijah lasted during the reign of Ahab King of Israel. The account of Ahab as king of Israel is found in I Kings 16:29-33. Elijah enters into the picture right afterwards in I Kings 17:1. Ahab is killed at the battle of Remote Gilead (I Kings 22:29-40). The narrative of the life of Elijah continues as he is taken up to heaven in a whirlwind as described in II Kings 2:1-12. According to the chronology completed by E.R. Thiele from his book *The mysterious numbers of the Hebrew kings*, Ahab ruled the northern nation of the Kingdom of Israel from 874-853 B.C. [F] John the Baptists ministry is estimated to have

emerged between 25-27 AD which will lead up to when Jesus was baptized. [G] So if you calculate the time when Elijah's prophetic ministry began to when John the Baptist started preaching in the wilderness it is about 900 years altogether.

[4] In the Old Testament when a third captain of the king's army approached Elijah he kneeled before him recognizing that the power of Elijah came from God. (II Kings 1:13-14) [J] Perhaps no one responded in this same manner but the symbolism between Elijah and John the Baptist in Scripture is divinely inspired by God. While Elijah and John the Baptist certainly had people that adamantly rejected their message they also had people whose eyes were opened to the truth and genuinely embraced their message and the power of the ministry as coming from the LORD.

[5] Matthew, Mark, and Luke each quote from Isaiah but don't quote John stating this about himself. The Gospel of John has John the Baptist stating that he is "the voice of one calling in the desert" (Isaiah 40:3).

[6] *Karpos* is the Greek noun used for the word fruit. This noun is used in throughout the New Testament. Some famous examples include the Parable of the Sower (Matthew 13:8, Mark 4:8, Luke 8:8), the command of Jesus while on His way to Jerusalem to not allow a specific fig tree to bear fruit again (Matthew 21:19), Parable of the tenants (Matthew 21:34, Mark 12:2, Luke 20:10) and the Vine and the Branches (John 15:2). Altogether this noun is used 66 times in the New Testament. The message of John the Baptist is consistent with the message of Jesus Christ and the Apostles. As Christians the fruit of the Gospel is to be evident in our lives.

[7] In the synoptic gospels account there is no record of a Pharisee named Simon who was conflicted between returning with the religious leaders or accepting the message of John the Baptist. When looking at examples like Nicodemus we do know that there would have been tremendous pressure on religious leaders not to accept the teachings of John the Baptist and then Jesus. This is a reminder for us today not to succumb to the pressures from the world and instead embrace the message of the Gospel.

[8] The Venerable Bede, the English monk of the 7th and 8th centuries stated, "It is evident that John not only preached, but also gave to some the baptism of repentance, but he could not give the baptism for the remission of sins. For the remissions of sins is only given to us by the baptism of Christ." [N]

[9] "Confessing their sins" was part of what was required for those who went to John the Baptist to be baptized. (Matthew 3:6, Mark 1:5). The Greek verb which is used is *exomo*logeo and is used a total of ten times in the New Testament. Interestingly in its translation this word is used both

to describe confession (Acts 19:18, James 5:16) as well as describing praise or thanks (Matthew 11:25, Luke 10:21). This teaches us a valuable lesson that true confession of our sins and true thanksgiving and praise to God are connected.

[10] All four gospels record John the Baptist stating he was "unworthy" to loosen the sandals of the one that was coming after him. In the synoptic Gospels (Matthew 3:11, Mark 1:8, Luke 3:16) this was stated prior to baptizing Jesus. In the Gospel of John this statement was mentioned after the baptism of Jesus to questioning Pharisees (John 1:27). We can conclude John probably made this statement at least twice. Upon seeing Jesus, John proceeds

[11] We don't know the exact details of when John the Baptist went into the Judean Wilderness just like we don't know when his parents passed away. Our Gospel accounts don't share when Zacharias and Elizabeth died but the fact that they were older when Elizabeth conceived him, we can rationalize that neither was alive when the ministry of John the Baptist began. We see so many similarities between Jesus and John the Baptist. They both are products of miraculous births, they are the only individuals in the New Testament to have a narrative about the events leading up to their conception and birth, they both fulfilled Old Testament prophecies, they are both prophets, John the Baptists father and Jesus' adoptive father were not mentioned in Scripture during their ministries, and Jesus and John were both put to death by political rulers whose authority came from Rome as they were governing their respective regions

[12] While we obviously don't know what the conversation was like between John and his family after returning from seeing John the Baptist and becoming his disciple, nowhere does it imply that James was a disciple of John nor do we see James as following Jesus during the early part of Jesus' ministry described in John's Gospel (John 1:35-4:54) but James was among the first four to follow Jesus as his full time disciples.

[13] The transliteration for the word wilderness is the Hebrew noun *midbar*. This word has been translated to both "wilderness" as well as "desert" (Deuteronomy 32:10). This noun was used to describe the desert/wilderness location of Joseph when tossed in the cistern (Genesis 37:22), Moses and the burning bush (Exodus 3:1) the desert of Sinai where Mount Sinai is located and where he received the Ten Commandments (Exodus 19:1 & 2), David as a shepherd (I Samuel 17:28) while hiding from King Saul (I Samuel 23:14 -15, 25:1, & 26:3) and also hiding from his son Absalom (II Samuel 15:28) and Elijah when fleeing from Jezebel (I Kings 19:4) to name a few.

Chapter 4

The Baptizer and the Messiah

Matthew 3:13-17; 4:1-11-Mark 1:9-11; 12-13- Luke 3:21-22; 4:1-13

While I was working with James, my father, and the hired hands to catch our share of fish, Jesus was leaving Nazareth, travelling southeast going down the valley of Jezreel and continuing further south passed Salim, [A] making his way to John the Baptist. John would eventually move his ministry north to Aenon (John 3:22-23), but at this time, Jesus would journey past the springs of Aenon, [B] traveling along the Jordan Valley, which is geographically between the Sea of Galilee to the north and the Dead Sea to the south. [C] Jesus arrived at his destination, showing His approval of the ministry and of John the Baptist by Himself being baptized. What king travels to the location of his servant rather than summon the individual to come to him? I tell you, my children, I have lived under the authority of many rulers and authorities and this is the action of no ordinary king. This is the action of Jesus, the King of kings (I Timothy 6:15, Revelation 19:16), showing the humility of a servant (Philippians 2:7) and subsequently showing His approval of

John's baptism and personally becoming baptized as a man [D] despite having no sins from which He needed remission. John humbly resisted Jesus request by stating Jesus should baptize him instead (Matthew 3:14). Andrew and I heard John preach a "baptism of repentance" (Matthew 3:11, Mark 1:4, Luke 3:3). John humbly declared he was unworthy but obediently submitted to the request of Jesus to be baptized. Jesus wasn't confessing any of his own sins or showing Himself subservient to the role of John. Instead, Jesus was being baptized for the sake of righteousness. [E] Jesus "fulfilled all righteousness", observing every aspect of the Law that humanity was under, and showing all believers that we too can be unified with Him, first in death and then, ultimately in eternal life.[1] [F] "So before Jesus was crucified on our behalf, He was first baptized on our behalf" expressed Polycarp. "Jesus identified with us so that we could be covered in His righteousness"[2] added the Apostle John.

Later on, the Apostle John discussed how the Trinity was profoundly present at the Baptism of Jesus. How the Heavens opened and the Holy Spirit descended like a dove and came to Jesus, representing the spiritual grace given through baptism that is available to all believers. [G] Then a voice, the voice of God the Father stated, "This is my Son, whom I love; with Him I am well pleased."

"How remarkable", the Apostle John stated, "that at His baptism, when Jesus was showing He was united with us, the Trinity, the Godhead, showed that they were united together."

While the event of Jesus' baptism was not witnessed by John and Andrew[3], hearing the account from John the Baptist would resonate with these two young men throughout their ministries. At Jesus' baptism, when He was showing unity with us, the Trinity showed that they were united together. Once God the Father's voice spoke, this was further validation that the Messiah had come.[4]

Temptation of Jesus
Matthew 4:1-11; Mark 1:12-13; Luke 4:1-13

After offering a public act of solidarity with believers by being baptized, Jesus followed this through an act of solitude. Jesus was led by the Holy Spirit as He traveled west over the Jordan River, and then south until He reached His destination in the Judean Wilderness. Moses referred to this place as "Jeshimon" (Numbers 21:20; 23:28) which means "the devastation." [1] When Adam was tempted by Satan for the first time; the location was the beautiful and luscious setting of the Garden of Eden. For Jesus, the view was not of scenic beauty, but rather a dry and arid setting with dust hills being the view of the horizon. There was no person there to accompany Him, only wild beasts for intimidation (Mark 1:13) [5] Of all the epic duels in the history of humanity, never were the stakes so high or the combatants more contrasting: Jesus Christ, the Son of God, against his adversary Satan, the fallen angel, the being who went from worshipping God's Son to striving to destroy His mission. There was no room for error. For if Jesus were to falter ever so slightly, His mission would be a failure and humanity's hope would be lost. Satan would not delegate this battle to one of his lesser demons. Lucifer would battle Jesus himself, using all the tools at his disposal that he used to destroy countless lives, he would now use on Jesus Christ, Heaven's favorite son. Satan acted as a typical lion would; attacking your victim presumably at their weakest point, after Jesus appeared most vulnerable going forty days without food. Rest assured, this would have no influence on the outcome of this confrontation. God sustained Moses (Exodus 34:28; Deuteronomy 9:18) and Elijah (I Kings 19:7-9) for the same duration of time, and Jesus would share this common experience with the two men that would appear with Him on the mount of Transfiguration. Satan was meticulous and calculated with his attacks. Here is where Jesus would face, up to this point, His greatest test. [6]

Satan first attacked Jesus based on current circumstances, which was lack of food, while also questioning the true title of Jesus by using the word "if." Satan said to Jesus, "if you are the Son of God" (Matthew 4:3) Three times Satan tested Jesus, and three times Jesus answered Satan with Scripture quoting from the same book of the Bible. Only Jesus could fully fulfill the demands of the Law (Matthew 5:17; Galatians 3:21-25). Therefore, it should come as no surprise that Jesus answered each of Satan's attacks with Scripture from the book of Deuteronomy. Prior to the children of Israel leaving the wilderness and entering into the Promised Land, Deuteronomy was proclaimed to instruct the people to be obedient to the Law of God. [K] It is safe to say that one of the last things that Satan wanted to hear from this time of testing was anything from the book of Deuteronomy.

During this time of testing, Satan questioned if Jesus was the Son of God and then challenged Jesus to perform a series of tasks. This included turning stones into bread (Matthew 4:3), throwing Himself off the pinnacle of the Temple and caught by His angels (Matthew 4:5-6), and bowing down and worship Satan, at which time Jesus would be given all the kingdoms of the world (Matthew 4:8-9). For each of these temptations, Satan was challenging Jesus to not just prove that He was the Son of God but also that He was the fulfillment of what was prophesied in the Word of God.

"How so?" asked Papias.

"Teikon\little dear children", take a closer look at each test and see what comes to mind. First of all, turning stones into bread, where was Jesus?"

"In the wilderness" answered Papias.

"Exactly. Now, being in the wilderness and miraculously obtaining bread, does that strike any similarities to the history of the Hebrew people?"

"Well it seems reminiscent of manna being provided for the children of Israel while they were in the wilderness" answered Polycarp.

"Exactly right, my child, God told Moses that he would 'rain down bread from heaven' (Exodus 16:4), and manna was provided for God's people while they were in the wilderness. Moses was a prophet of God, and before he died he prophesied that God would "raise up a prophet for you like me from among you, from your fellow Israelites. You must listen to him." (Deuteronomy 18:15 NIV). By challenging Jesus to turn stones turn into bread, Satan wasn't just challenging Jesus as the Son of God, Satan was challenging Jesus as the prophet about whom Moses was speaking." [L]

"Now, the next test to which Satan would subject our Savior also required a new visual location. Instead of the physical need of eating bread in the wilderness, Satan was attacking the pride and identity of Jesus. Satan brought Jesus to the pinnacle of the Temple. Here the highest point of the Temple was directly over the Kidron Valley which was an awe-inspiring 450-foot drop. [N]

Here was Satan once again testing Jesus, this time in Jerusalem, the city in the center of many nations (Ezekiel 5:5), and in the Temple, the center of Jewish religious activities, customs, and festivals. This time, Satan did not question if Jesus was truly a prophet, but if He was really a...."

"Priest" was the immediate reply of an excited Papias.

"Excellent my son. The temptation occurred at the Temple, and the book of Hebrews is very clear that Jesus is our high priest (Hebrews 4:14-16). The Psalmist David described the Messiah as a priest when he wrote, "The LORD hath sworn and will not repent, Thou art a priest for ever after the order of Melchizedek." (Psalm 110:4 KJV).So Satan was questioning Jesus, "Are you really a priest? Are you really who King David was writing about in that Psalm? If so prove it to me, jump off the pinnacle of the Temple, and the angels will not let you fall 450 feet to your death. IF...all that is true, and Satan even quoted from a Psalm to get his point across (Psalm 91:11-12). Jesus answered in a most profound manner. As the Son of God, as high priest, and as the Messianic fulfillment of Scripture, Jesus was not subject to the authority of Satan. Jesus once again quoted from Deuteronomy (6:16) and passed the second test because He was not subjected to the authority or commands of Satan. Jesus was an eternal priest, in the order of Melchizedek (Hebrews 5:6).

Lastly, Satan now took Jesus to a mountain for one final test. Here was where Satan, the 'god of this age' (II Corinthians 4:4) would tempt Jesus with the wealth of this world. For this final test I found it interesting that Satan did not address Jesus as "Son of God." Perhaps, by bringing this up, Satan worried that Jesus would be reminded of the vast superiority of the splendors of heaven. I was Blessed to see part of the heavenly glory (Revelation 4), and there is nothing that could make me forget that splendor. Heaven was formerly the residence for Satan and he understands earthly kingdoms are but the smallest fraction of what heaven offers. Satan chose not to mention that Jesus was the Son of God. Yet by taking Jesus on a mountain, perhaps Satan was tempting Jesus by implying Jesus could freely have all this without the need of suffering like He would on Calvary. Jesus, descendant of

David, (Psalm 89:3-4; Jeremiah 23:5-6; 33:15-16) was shown the kingdoms of the world, and Satan stated that Jesus could be given them if He worshipped Satan. By implying, "If you're a king, where is your kingdom?" Satan tempted Jesus by offering Him one. Jesus told Pontius Pilate, 'My kingdom is not of this world' (John 18:36). Jesus did not have to prove to Satan that He was truly a King, Satan already knew, but he still tempted Jesus with the best that this world has to offer, and worshipping Satan to obtain worldly riches was never a consideration of our Savior. Instead, Jesus quoted from Deuteronomy for the third time (6:13) Prophet, Priest and King (Matthew 4:11; Mark 1:13). God's preeminent[7] Son, Jesus Christ, was brought into the world and all God's angels worshipped and served Him (Hebrews 1:6).

Modern Day Application

John the Baptist, a man of priestly lineage, was so charismatic and engaging that people from all over Palestine were willing to travel to the Jordan River to hear him speak. Imagine the following that John would have received if he used his personality for selfish measures and attracted crowds of people in Jerusalem or Alexandria or some other metropolitan area with a high population of Jews. Yet John wasn't preaching out of selfish ambition but rather obedience to his calling to prepare the way for the Messiah despite the challenging road he was forced to walk. Jesus was given an opportunity by Satan to avoid the challenges, suffering and shame that lay before Him in ministry and eventually the cross. Avoiding greed and materialism as well as devotion to a state that wasn't the Kingdom of God were both paths refused by John the Baptist and Jesus. With that in mind let us look at the life of Aleksandr Isayevich Solzhenitsyn. Solzhenitsyn was born into adversity with his father having died six months prior to his birth in a hunting accident. [O] Solzhenitsyn fought for the Soviet Union during World War II as the Allies sought to end the atrocities committed by Hitler and the Nazi party. When people think of the horrors of the 20th century the first name that typically comes to mind is Adolph Hitler. Yet where Solzhenitsyn makes a name for himself is by using his gift of writing to expose the heinous acts committed by Stalin and the USSR post World War II. Solzhenitsyn spent eight years in a labor camp in the frigid Arctic islands for criticizing Joseph Stalin in a letter to a friend. After completing his sentence Solzhenitsyn was then sent into what was described as "permanent exile." It was during this time that Solzhenitsyn's was drawn deeper into Christianity. If Solzhenitsyn wanted to make his life easy he certainly could have dedicated himself to writing favorably of the USSR with the hopes that a man of his considerable talent could be richly used by the USSR. Or promised to be a "good citizen" for the communist regime and simply look the other way when the iron first of communism continues to dominate and destroy their own. Instead Solzhenitsyn was a man of conviction and his faith in God and his abhorrence towards injustice caused for his words to get worldwide attention.

Eventually the USSR had enough and deported Solzhenitsyn where he eventually resided in Vermont. One might think that upon his arrival to the United States he would have nothing but glowing remarks for his new home. However, while glaringly different from the USSR the United States had discernible issues that Solzhenitsyn felt convicted to expose. Solzhenitsyn was given the platform as the commencement speaker for Harvard University in 1978 and he chose to expose the shortcomings of both the USSR as well as the United States. While communism and its limited freedom pushed for the state to be respected above all, even God, this damaged the church in the East. The West had a different threat. Materialism, greed, moral decline, and commercial interests were all causing irrevocable damage to the Western World, specifically the United States. [P] This was in 1978. Imagine what he would say today? Jesus, John the

Baptist, and Aleksandr Isayevich Solzhenitsyn were not primarily interested in taking the easy road. Their concern was to speak what is true and be obedient to their calling. Materialism, greed, and devotion to Rome were not the primary motivations of Jesus or John the Baptist but rather devotion towards the Kingdom of God. May the church be likeminded in our commitment.

Chapter 4 Footnotes

[1] Romans 6:4-5 "We were therefore buried with Him through baptism into death in order that, just as Christ was raised from the dead through the glory of the Father, we too may live a new life. If we have been united with Him like this in His death, we will certainly also be united with Him in His resurrection." (NIV) In this verse we see the Apostle Paul describes the historical events of the death of Jesus, His burial and also His Resurrection. In verse 5 the Apostle Paul states the unity we have Christ in His death, or as Stott states, "with Him in the likeness of His death." [H]

[2] II Corinthians 5:21-For He made Him who had no sin to be sin for us, that we might become the righteousness of God in Him ." (NKJV)

[3] The Baptist of Jesus is described in Matthew, Mark and Luke as part of the narrative. However, in the Gospel of John the baptism of Jesus is described in past tense when John the Baptist gave testimony about the Holy Spirit descending as a dove (John 1:32-34). After John the Baptist told this story Jesus reemerges and John the Baptist points Andrew and John to Jesus as the Lamb of God (John 1:35). We are given no indication in any of the Gospels that Andrew and John were present at the baptism of Jesus. One logical explanation is that Andrew and John were followers of John the Baptist but would also return to Galilee and therefore they were not present when Jesus was baptized

[4] Psalm 2:7 and Isaiah 42:7 are both Messianic verses and descriptive imagery in these prophetic verses are seen in the baptism of Jesus from Psalm 2:7- "I will proclaim the decree of the LORD: He said to me, 'You are my Son; today I have become your Father" to this statement in Isaiah 42:1, "my chosen one in whom I delight; I will put my Spirit on him."

[5] Of the three Gospels that describe the testing of Jesus in the wilderness, the Gospel of Mark, which is the shortest narrative, is the only mention of there being wild animals. This reference, besides being historically accurate, seems to be included for a few reasons. A student of the Old Testament might be reminded of Job 5:22b-23- "And need not fear the beasts of the earth. For you will have a covenant with the stones of the field, and the wild animals will be at peace with you." (NIV). Secondly, one of the primary ways of martyrdom for the early church was being tossed to wild animals. This happened to believers during the reign of Nero (54-68 AD) but also much afterwards including the martyrdom of Ignatius during the reign of Trajan (98-117 AD) [J] For the believer going through these trials they could find encouragement that Jesus went through them to and that He "overcame the world" (John 16:33)

[6] Here the word for "tempt" as used in Matthew 4:1 is *peirazein*. This can mean either "to tempt" or "to test." [M]

[7] In Hebrews 1:6 we see that Jesus is described as God's "firstborn." The adjective that is used there is *prototokos* which is translated "first-born" but can also be translated to mean "eldest" or "pre-eminent." (biblehub.com)

Chapter 5

Fishermen Follow Jesus

John 1:28-42
From Disciples of John to Disciples of Jesus and then get Peter

Andrew and I eagerly anticipated rejoining John the Baptist and his ministry. For each question we could answer it seemed two more emerged. Peter would join us for part of the journey but not to see John the Baptist, for he had other affairs to manage. Once again, Andrew and I, the younger brothers, would not be accompanied by the firstborn of our families, Peter and James respectively, to see John the Baptist. Hopefully some of our questions would be answered by the Baptizer, but what we faced was nothing compared to the bombardment that John was facing while in Bethany.[1] How perplexed they were with this ministry of the son of a priest. Perhaps these priests and Levites hoped to still convince him to take on the duty of his ancestors and become a priest. One could only become a priest based entirely on descent and lineage, and since this was the only qualification, one could not become disqualified for any other reason. [A] The religious authorities preferred for John to be an ally rather than an adversary, yet the purpose of John's calling would occur the next day when Jesus of Nazareth would come to John at Bethany.

John would go from justifying his ministry to proclaiming its purpose when he saw Jesus approaching, pointed and proclaimed to all who were present, "Behold, the Lamb of God, who takes away the sin of the world!" (John 1:29b ESV). Priests were accustomed to handling lambs as part of the sacrificial duty. One might have thought that, by not embracing the role of a priest in Jerusalem, John the Baptist would not be required to have any roles with lambs. This was most certainly not the case. For when the prophet Isaiah wrote, "He was opposed, and He was afflicted, Yet He did not open His mouth, like a lamb that is led to slaughter" (Isaiah 53:7a NAS), John the Baptist was prophetically stating to all present, that Jesus is the Lamb of God, offered as a sacrifice by God, on behalf of man. Andrew and I were not present for this first public declaration by the prophet John, but we would be there for the second.

John the Baptist gave Jesus public affirmation right before Jesus completes His time of temptation in the wilderness, where His purpose and identity was questioned while in isolation. Now, His purpose and identity would be proclaimed in exaltation to a crowd of witnesses.

"So to recap, just so that we are on the same page" chimed in Polycarp. "On the first day John the Baptist was questioned by priests and Levites from Jerusalem (John 1:19-28). Then, after they left, the very next day is when Jesus arrived at Bethany" (John 1:29-34).

"Correct", affirmed the Apostle. "And then on the third day is when Andrew and I arrived with our intent to be with John the Baptist (John 1:35-42). This reunion of sorts was shorter than we would have expected because God's plan was for us to be with Jesus at the onset of His ministry. As we arrived, we didn't hear John delivering a fiery discourse. Instead, he spotted us right away and came over to greet us, and his demeanor was noticeably different.

"So much has changed since we have last seen each other, I am practically at a loss for words!" exclaimed John. "My ministry was never about me; this was never about my name. My ministry was always about the one whom would come after me, and He has come!"

Andrew and I were stunned at what we were hearing. John the Baptist, the first prophet in over four and a half centuries was struggling to find the words when explaining about the one who was coming after him.

Then it happened. John stated for the second day in a row upon seeing Jesus, "Look the Lamb of God!"

Andrew and I turned around at practically the same time but with very different reactions. Andrew was intrigued, I was dumbfounded, for once again I found myself looking at a man of prophetic fulfillment and I was related to him. We didn't say anything loudly at first, just quietly to each other.

"Who is he?" Andrew quietly asked.

"Jesus of Nazareth", I replied. "He is my Aunt Mary's son."

"Are you related to everybody?" Andrew replied, in what appeared to be more of a stunned reply than sarcasm. Jesus was looking at us waiting for a response while Andrew and I stood there each hoping the other would speak up.

Finally, Jesus broke the awkward silence and said, "What do you want?"

Now, think about this scenario for just a moment, John the Baptist was the first prophet in about 450 years emphatically shared the primary reason for his service was to prepare the way for the one who is coming after him and this person is of far greater relevance and importance than the prophet John the Baptist. Oh yeah, and this person is my relative Jesus. Here was my opportunity to say anything to him, something deep, profound, personal, but instead the words that came out of my mouth were, "Rabbi, where are you staying?"[2] Despite the unimpressive dialogue on my end this didn't stop Jesus from giving a genuine invitation as his first words says everything you need to know about His heart for us.

"Come", was His reply, "and you will see."

Little did I know that accepting this invitation would pave the way to witness God restoring His relationship with humanity. This moment changed my eternity, and it was the tenth hour (this is 4:00 in the afternoon for our time) John, the prophet, no longer needed to proclaim what would come to pass but rather who has arrived. Pointing people towards Jesus was the purpose for the ministry of John the Baptist. As a result, for me personally, John became a bridge allowing me to go from being a fisherman in my father's business to becoming a disciple of the Messiah.

As the three of us walked along to where Jesus was staying, one might suppose that doubts would have come to my mind before Andrew's. After all, Jesus was from my family, how would the Messiah come from a person who was related to me? At least with John the Baptist, he came from a family of priests; Jesus came from a poor carpenter's family [D] in what was presumed the most insignificant town of Galilee. Yet never in the course of the conversation between Jesus, Andrew, and me did it appear that the man we were following was destined to live out His days in a carpenter's shop. Going from being part of the crowds listening to John the Baptist to walking along with a group of three was a major shift, but one which I found more fulfilling as we walked with Jesus through Perea to where He was staying. After we arrived at our destination, Andrew, in his excitement realized that his brother Simon (Peter) was not far from this location. Immediately, Andrew exclaimed that he wanted to go get his brother and bring him to Jesus, [3] which was warmly received by Jesus. In many ways, the ministerial work of Andrew began when he brought his brother to see Jesus. Andrew in Greek means "manly," [E] and all men who are followers of Jesus should strive to be as bold as Andrew by continuing bringing people to Jesus, for that defined his ministry. My reaction was one which would come to define my time during the ministry of Jesus and that was to remain close to my LORD.

My time alone with Jesus was treasured immediately. Jesus was my earthly relative, but I didn't yet recognize that He was also my heavenly Savior. Mystery surrounded Jesus in my family due to the seemingly less than auspicious beginning of the marriage of Joseph and Mary, yet there was always a sense that there was so much more to Jesus than anyone realized. While waiting for Andrew and Simon, I had a sense that perhaps I would unlock the mystery of my older cousin, but that notion quickly dissipated, and I found myself enjoying His company. We talked about family, told stories, we laughed together, and while I didn't know why, I knew that this was where I was supposed to be. In these early moments, Jesus didn't share with me the mysteries of the Gospel, the truth of the Trinity, or the wonders of heaven because I was not ready for this depth of knowledge. Instead, Jesus did something far greater in our time together; He showed me that He loved me, right from the start. God's love was present during our fellowship and it was then that I realized that wherever Jesus was, that is where I wanted to be.

Andrew successfully returned bringing his brother to Jesus after proclaiming to him, "We have found the Messiah" (John 1:41). In all my years with Peter, I never asked him what he was expecting after hearing this proclamation from his brother. Individuals in elevated positions typically make things about themselves, and there was no position any Jewish person at this time anticipated more than the arrival of the Messiah. Yet upon entering the residence, Jesus didn't explain His credentials; instead, He changed Simon Peter's identity with the first words he ever spoke to him. Before even exchanging greetings, Jesus referred to how the world viewed him, "Simon, son of Jonah." Jesus then continued, "You will be called Cephas" (Peter).[4] This pronouncement on the part of Jesus wasn't done after an extensive discussion with Simon Peter or after Andrew and I had extensively validated him as a man of character and leadership. The reality was that nobody had described him this way until it was declared by Jesus.

Adding two more to our three
John 1:43-51

So there I was with Simon Peter and Andrew, which wasn't outside of the norm, but instead of being on a fishing boat, we were walking with the prophesied Messiah. "Three fishermen and the Son of God were walking down the road" sounds like a line from a Greek comedy rather than a historical event in Galilee. Speaking of Greek and fisherman, while on our journey with Jesus, we ran into Philip of Bethsaida, a Jewish fisherman with a Greek name.[5] While we personally knew Philip the eyes of Jesus were fixated on the young Galilean who was a combination of Hebrew and Greek influence. [F] Philip almost looked startled when he saw Jesus gazing in his direction and then perplexed to see the three of us with Him.

"Follow me" was the simple, life changing offer Jesus gave to Philip. No interview process, no examining of his qualifications, Jesus purely stated to Philip, "Follow me."

Philip then looked over at the three of us, Andrew gave a smile and nodded his head in a gesture of assurance, and, with that, our group now consisted of four followers. During our conversation, it became quickly apparent we weren't in the presence of a typical carpenter. Jesus was sharing truths that made Philip rationalize that perhaps Jesus was the fulfillment of Scripture going all the way back to the Torah. Jesus then looked over at Philip and said, "Is there anything that you want to ask me?"

Philip thought about it for a moment before asking, "Where are you from?"

"Nazareth" replied Jesus.

"Is that where we are going?"

"No, we have other plans" smiled Jesus in reply. "We have a wedding to attend in Cana." "Really? Cana?" replied Philip. "I have a close friend who lives in Cana." [6]

"Yes I know you do", grinned Jesus. "He is invited to join us, feel free to invite him." [7]

"Yes Rabbi" stated Philip excitedly and with that he was off to find Nathaniel, as if seeking to fulfill his first assignment as a follower of Jesus.

"Nathaniel," shouted Philip as soon as he was within shouting distance. Nathaniel was surprised to see Philip and confused at the level of excitement he was exhibiting. Philip was sprinting towards Nathaniel to get to him as quickly as possible. Gasping for air through excitement and exhaustion Philip exclaimed, "We have found the one Moses wrote about in the Law, and about whom the prophets also wrote- Jesus of Nazareth, the son of Joseph."

Understandably Nathaniel's response was skepticism rather than excitement. "Can anything good come out of Nazareth?" Personally I can picture Nathaniel thinking, "How gullible must people from Bethsaida be that they would so quickly follow someone from Nazareth?"[8] Peter and Andrew were originally from Bethsaida before moving to Capernaum, [9] and now Philip, also from Bethsaida, was trying to convince Nathaniel to follow a man from Nazareth.

"Lack of faith" voiced Polycarp.

"Agreed" stated Papias as the two you young students of the Apostle waited for confirmation of their consensus.

"Before anyone becomes to disparaging over the skeptical response of Nathaniel, his viewpoint wasn't without merit. If anything, his initial pessimism showed that Nathaniel had a strong knowledge of the Scriptures, as he spent countless hours studying in the synagogue. Nathaniel remembered the words of the prophet Micah, "But you, O Bethlehem Ephrathah, who are too little to be among the clans of Judah, from you shall come forth for me one who is to be ruler in

Israel, whose coming forth is from of old, from ancient days" (Micah 5:2 ESV).

We know that our Savior Jesus Christ was born in Bethlehem and fulfilled this prophecy, but Philip never mentioned this, so the uncertainty of his response was for good reason. Yet Nathaniel wasn't deterred from seeing for himself, so he went with Philip to meet Jesus.

As Philip and Nathaniel were approaching Jesus, Peter, Andrew and myself, Jesus didn't employ a standard pitch to convince people to become His followers. Instead Jesus treated the people on an individual basis. For Andrew and myself, the first words Jesus spoke was asking us what we wanted. For Peter, Jesus immediately changed his name. Philip was given the immediate invitation to "Follow me." While Nathaniel was unsure who Jesus was, the first words that Jesus spoke revealed He had knowledge of Nathaniel. Jesus said to him, "Here is a true[10] Israelite, in whom there is nothing false" (John 1:47b NIV).

Nathaniel was stunned as he expected the same invitation that Philip received, "Follow me." This was certainly a topic of discussion among the two while they travelled to see Jesus. Jesus showed Nathaniel instantly that He was more than just a common man from Nazareth. Nathaniel looked at

Philip who simply shrugged his shoulders so as to gesture he didn't know how Jesus knew anything about him.

"How do you know me?" Nathaniel asked as he was clearly taken back.

"I saw you while you were still under the fig tree[11] before Philip called you." Now we were all confused.

"How did Jesus see him? Philip and Nathaniel were ahead of us" I said quietly while leaning over to Peter and Andrew. Peter shook his head and simply said, "This is not an ordinary man." Nathaniel shared those sentiments after Jesus conveyed knowledge supernaturally that Nathaniel presumed could only have been known by himself. His doubts were gone without any concern to his prior objections. Nathaniel proclaimed all at once that Jesus was a teacher, God's Son, and the King of Israel. Nathaniel went from skeptic to follower in mere moments. This capped an indescribable few days. Two days earlier, John the Baptist declared that Jesus was "the Lamb of God" (John 1:35). Later on that day, Andrew declared to his brother that Jesus was "the Messiah" (John 1:41). Then, the following day, Philip proclaimed that Jesus was the fulfillment of prophecy, and Nathaniel declared Jesus as God's Son all in a two-day span.

Jesus assured Nathaniel the best was yet to come when he stated, "Truly, truly,[12] I say to you, you will see heaven opened, and the angels of God ascending and descending on the Son of Man." (John 1:51 ESV) Jesus never had to extend an invitation to Nathaniel, he simply started following Jesus. We were all in awe of Jesus after just two days, and we didn't even see a miracle yet. This would occur the following day.

First Year of Ministry for Jesus

John 2:1-12

Jesus Turns Water into Wine

Eight miles! This is no significant distance, not even half a day's journey. Yet these miles spoke wonders. The difference between acceptance and rejection, openness and closed-mindedness, revelation and reluctance, signs and self-seeking, this was the difference between Cana and Nazareth. These 8 miles presented an opportunity for Jesus to reveal Himself through a sign. Nazareth, the hometown of Jesus, was not open to Jesus being anything more than a carpenter's son. Nazareth may have watched Jesus grow up but it is remarkable how little they knew about the man who would change the world. So instead of occurring in Nazareth, the first sign given by Jesus would be eight miles north in Cana .N 13

Nazareth's lack of faith was Cana's gain, and due to the providence of God, I was one of five individuals who had a unique vantage point. What an unlikely handful we were: Simon, who was now named Peter, and his younger brother and fishing partner Andrew; Philip, the man who had a Greek name but loved the Hebrew Scriptures, who was from Bethsaida, made up of mostly Gentiles but built under the authority of Herod the Great; O Nathaniel also known Bartholomew, [14] the man with two names but a singular focus, particularly when it came to Scripture; and yours truly John, last but not least, actually maybe the least, the youngest of the five and the youngest son of Zebedee. Unique doesn't begin to describe us; well, besides the fact that all five of us were fishermen. We were identical in that aspect. Five fishermen following a carpenter wouldn't appear compelling. Yet this story isn't chronicled because Jesus was a carpenter; it's because He is the Messiah and our significance isn't found in who we were but rather who we were following, and it all started with a simple word, "Come."

While the five of us walked with Jesus towards Cana to attend the wedding, the mere fact that we adhered to the command "Come" reverberated in my mind in a way that appeared to be far more fervent than seems logical. I felt a sense of pride, without understanding the justification for this emotion. Seeing the reaction of John the Baptist told me everything I needed to know in regard to whether or not I would be obedient to the call of Jesus. "Come". This most simple command on the part of Jesus became my focal point. As we travelled along it dawned on me that my brother James should be part of this as well. Just as Peter and Andrew were experiencing the beginnings of a profound movement, I longed for my brother James to be part of this as well.

My first experience as a follower of Jesus was far more enjoyable setting than my time following John the Baptist. This is meant as no disrespect to the prophetic ministry of John the Baptist, but a weeklong celebration at a wedding[15] was far more delightful than staying along the banks of the Jordan River. Upon arriving, Jesus was warmly greeted by many family members and close friends. Some of us felt a little out of place because we didn't know too many people. This wedding was for a relative of Jesus on Joseph, His adopted father's side. Since this was a family event for Jesus, it was accepted for him to arrive with the five of us.[16] Being from Cana, Nathaniel knew the most people at the wedding, besides Jesus of course. While I was in the midst of feeling like the ultimate tag, along I heard a familiar voice.

"Well I certainly didn't expect to see my sister's youngest son join us for this festive occasion." My Aunt Mary, the mother of Jesus stopped what she was doing to give me a warm greeting. "How are your parents and brother doing?" asked Mary genuinely.

"Everyone is doing well and business is going great; my father is always looking to expand." Unintentionally, my response could have come across as insensitive being as I was emphasizing the financial success of our family to my mothers' sister who was living in a significantly lower economic status, but being young, I always fell back on what I knew best and that was fishing. Mary's response couldn't have been any more gracious.

"Well as long as there are fish in the Sea of Galilee, Zebedee will find a way to catch them," she stated courteously.

"James, Joseph, Jude and Simon are all over there so be sure to say hello," stated Mary, referring to the brothers of Jesus before turning her attention back to Jesus.

"A mother knows" is a simple but insightful saying. In those early moments, seeing my Aunt Mary look at Jesus and then the five of us, while she didn't know the exact details, she recognized that we were on the cusp of something.

Weddings were quite the elaborate presentation. First we watched as the groom revealed himself along with selected friends outside of his home. While the groom waited by his home during the evening a parade of people came down the streets. [R] People cheered as torches were lit, singers sang, dancers danced, all while we were anticipating seeing the bride. Applause peaked after the bride was revealed to the groom and all those in attendance. Selected individuals gave speeches, the groom took the bride to his home, and despite all the pomp and circumstance that the day had already offered, the spectacle was far from complete.[17]

Peter, Andrew, Philip and Nathaniel took the opportunity to mingle with the different guests at the wedding. Unsurprisingly, my actions foreshadowed the next three and a half years of my life which was remaining close by Jesus' side. After a few days of complete merriment Jesus' mother came over to us with a look of concern. Jesus, noticing that she was flustered went over to talk to her away from the guests. Naturally, I tagged along and the other four, not wanting to be outdone joined Jesus who was with his mother and the servants of the wedding.

"They have no more wine"[18] (John 2:3b NIV) stated Mary, whose prominent role at a family wedding allowed for her to be privy to information only known by a select few at this time. There was a collective gasp by the other four recognizing the seriousness of the matter while my eyes immediately became fixated on Jesus. Hospitality was a sacred duty among the Hebrew people, particularly at a wedding. [U] The degree of embarrassment and shame that would have come on the couple, particularly the family of the groom, was substantial and highly worrisome. Two questions immediately came to mind. Why was Jesus' mother telling Jesus this concerning information? Was there anything that Jesus could do?

I felt a sickening feeling for the embarrassment that would occur for the groom and his family and I felt sympathy for my Aunt Mary as she was feeling distraught for people whom she loved. What I wasn't feeling was hopeful that there was anything that Jesus could do to meet the need. Regrettably I had no answers, only questions. So I, along with the other disciples, the servants at the wedding, and my Aunt Mary, all responded in same manner, we looked to Jesus.

"Woman[19] what have I to do with thee?[20] My hour has not yet come."[21] (KJV)

Listening to Jesus and the apparent hesitancy to intervene I didn't know how my Aunt Mary was hoping her son would respond. Practical measures were quietly discussed among the five of us. "Is there anywhere we could buy more wine? Do we have any money?" Philip asked quietly to the rest of us.[22]

Mary didn't respond or even acknowledge our side conversation as she was completely transfixed on Jesus. Mary didn't have a clue what was about to take place but there was something in the interchange between mother and son that she had peace leaving this problem in the hands of Jesus.

"Do whatever he tells you" Mary stated to the servants[23] that were working the wedding and she then proceeded to make her way to mingle with the guests and act in a manner that everything was running smoothly.

Upon Mary exiting, servants focused their attention upon Jesus, who, in mere moments, went from being a normal guest to the source of hope for a desperate family and concerned servants. Jesus was a picture of calm despite the anxiety that was evident for everyone involved.

"Fill the jars with water," Jesus stated in a composed fashion. I looked over to see six stone jars[24] in the one corner of the room. Without hesitation the servants began the task of filling up each of the jars.

"That's about 150 gallons" stated Andrew to the four of us after quickly doing the math in his head.

We were nothing more than bystanders at this time. These six jars were customarily used for Jewish rites of purification. In the Old Testament God stressed the importance of His people being ritually clean and separate from the contamination of sin. [X] Purification was done in obedience to God with the expectation that God would deliver His people from their enemies. These jars were used by Jewish people to wash their hands prior to eating a meal, otherwise they would be ceremonially unclean. [Y] This particular ceremonial cleansing was not part of the Law of God as recorded by Moses or any other prophet but rather laws that were added by Jewish religious leaders and tradition would dictate that this type of washing be adhered to by followers of Judaism.

"Was their anything in these six jars at this time?" asked Polycarp.

"No my son" answered the Apostle and eyewitness to this first sign. "At this time these jars were also empty symbolically representing that the resources of God's people had been exhausted. [Z] God's plan of restoration and fulfillment was being illustrated before our very eyes in this first sign. Without the intervention of Jesus this wedding celebration would cease once it was realized that the resources were consumed and culturally embarrassment and shame would befall upon the family.

After filling completing the first command of Jesus the servants were waiting for further instructions. They had done exactly as commanded; the pots were filled to the very top with water, and there was no room to add anything else to the jars without them spilling over.

Then Jesus gave a command which nobody expected, "Now draw some out and take it to the master of the feast" (John 2:8b ESV). Nobody voiced a word of concern but it was written all over everyone's faces. Wine was typically diluted to varying degrees to keep people from the sin of drunkenness but this wine wasn't watered down, it was just water. Apprehension was the understandable emotion of the servants as they didn't want to appear foolish nevertheless they were obedient to the command of Jesus. Calmly I walked from the room of service to watch the reaction of the master of the banquet when he tasted what I presumed was still water. Surprise came over his face, but unforeseen to me, it was delight not disappointment. I watched as he motioned for the groom to make his way over to him, so I quickly made my way in that direction so as to hear the conversation. Praise was his response not displeasure as he stated to the groom, "Every man at the beginning sets out the good wine, and when the guests have well drunk, then the inferior. You have kept the good wine until now!" (John 2:10 NKJV).

In retrospect, this first sign shows us much more than providing wine at a wedding. Jesus had mastery over the elements because He is the creator of all things.[25] Additionally, considering the audience most people would have chosen to have different individuals present for this first miracle of Jesus. This sign wasn't performed in the city of Jerusalem in front of the religious leaders but rather in Cana, a town of Galilee. Jesus didn't call back the honored guests so individuals considered more prestigious would witness this act of greatness. Jesus audience for his first sign was limited to fishermen and servants. This is reminiscent to the angels of heaven announcing the birth of Jesus not to those in exalted political or religious positions but rather shepherds. Additionally, this first sign showed us a lot about the work of God. Jesus easily could have made wine that was equivalent to what had already been consumed or done what is customary and offered a lesser wine as was customary for that point of the celebration. In this first sign Jesus displayed that the standards of God are far superior to the standards of man.

27 AD - First Passover of Ministry

John 2:12-25

James, Joseph, Judas and Simeon, who were the brothers of Jesus,[26] were not present for the proclamation about John the Baptist pertaining to Jesus and they weren't present when Jesus turned the water into wine. When the popularity of Jesus would grow the seed of resentment would be planted in their hearts. At this particular time, however, there was not a hint of animosity on the part of Jesus' brother to the rest of us present. In fact, the number of people who were with Jesus as he was leaving Cana literally doubled as his four brothers and mother accepted the gracious invite on the part of Peter to join them at his house in Capernaum. Everyone seemed genuinely excited to be together but I was reflecting more on what I had seen than contemplating who I was with. As we prepared to exit Cana, I turned and saw one of the servants who was obedient to Jesus and helped fill the six stone water pots. He was gazing in our direction. I sensed he was yearning to be part of the group as he no doubt wondered what was yet to come. He saw me looking at him and we acknowledged one another and then I continued on my journey. What I am sure this servant failed to realize at this time, along with the rest of us, is that we didn't just witness the power of God, we witnessed the beginning of a new movement by God, one in which Jesus revealed that the Jewish ceremonial washings were going to be replaced.[27] While Jesus used jars for ceremonial washings to reveal His glory, God would use the death of His son to make us spiritually clean in a way that a ceremonial washing never could. [AA]

After spending a few days with Peter and his family and since Passover time was near (Deuteronomy 16:16) we began our trek up to Jerusalem.[28] Since my Father owned a house in Jerusalem for the business we were able to stay there. Upon arriving in the city we made our way to the Temple. Passover was always a chaotic time of year in Jerusalem and to describe the city as "a little packed" is like describing the Dead Sea "a little salty." Jews from three separate continents all descended upon the city and in the midst of the chaos on the streets we made our way to the Temple.

Walking up the twelve steps made of Corinthian brass to entering into the Temple through the eastern gate, which is the main entrance into the Temple and is commonly referred to as the beautiful gate. [CC] This gate required 20 men to open and close the double doors due to its massive size and the majestic tone set the standard for the Temple to truly be one of the architectural triumphs of the century. For the five of us the sight of the Temple was always an experience, for Jesus he appeared unimpressed but the outward splendor and beauty because He could clearly see that something was missing. Certainly there was no need for additional marble pillars another spectacular gate. What the Temple was missing was leaders with genuine devotion in service to the LORD. Annas[29], the former high priest, set the standard in this department and a majority of the individuals in positions of authority followed his lead. The Temple had become less about praise and more about profit. After entering through the beautiful gate we emerged into the Court of Gentiles. In the midst of the beauty and grandeur the ethnic divide was visible with a 54-inch Marble screen with Greek and Latin inscriptions warning non-Jews that to proceed would mean death.[30] Jews and Gentiles could only fellowship together in the outer enclosure which was a square of 750 feet. Upon reaching this location it seemed like practically every inch was occupied by either travelers or individuals seeking to exploit them. Annas and his sons capitalized on those who made a pilgrimage to Jerusalem and substantially increased their wealth as a result. Cattle, sheep, and doves were being sold inside the gates of the Temple, particularly in the Court of Gentiles. Devoted Jews who came to Jerusalem and paid their Temple tax (Exodus 30:13-14; II Chronicles 24:9) were making money changers rich in the process. Someone travelling from Alexandria or Syria for example, would have different currency so they had to change their money either into Jewish or Tyrian because their coins had a high degree of purity in silver. DD Here the Temple courtyard resembled more of a marketplace than a place of worship.

Unfortunately, those that would travel to Jerusalem on an annual basis were desensitized to the lack of reverence towards God in an atmosphere that seemed to be primarily focused on greed. Is this what an individual born into a Gentile family was to believe was proper worship for the God of the Jews? Why would anyone find this appealing? Jesus became incensed with the disdain shown by the priesthood towards the Holiness of God, worship of YHWH, and sacred attitude towards His Father. Lots of noise and commotion was taking place with sheep and oxen moaning, and money changers clicking their coins together to let people know they were ready for business.EE While the commerce of the courtyard was thriving, the holy intent of the Temple, which was worship, prayer, and communion with God, had become practically non-existent.

Jesus couldn't tolerate the violation of His Father's house. While I was distracted by my surroundings unbeknownst to me Jesus was off to the side with several chords preparing for a cleansing. After hearing the lashing of a whip I turned around to witness a tumultuous scene as sheep and oxen were running in a chaotic manner, tables overturned, the sound of silver coins were clanging on the ground as the bedlam of scattering people and animals surrounded me. Nobody was hurt or even hit by the whip, for that was never the intent [GG] yet this didn't change the reality that Jesus singlehandedly cleared the courtyard of its corruptive actions. Despite having the numbers advantage, none of the money changers dared to challenge Him. When Jesus told them to leave they left.

"Get out of here! How dare you turn my Father's house into a market!" (John 2:16b NIV)

After these words thundered from the mouth of Jesus I backed into Philip and I turned around and the other four were standing there as stunned as I was.

"Zeal for your house will consume me" Nathaniel said in a quiet tone, and it was at that point we all recollected the words of the Psalmist David (Psalm 69:9a). This was not just a random event but the fulfillment of a prophecy written over

1,000 years ago by the man considered to be Israel's greatest king.

After the commotion had died down, after the last coin had fallen on its side, and after the shrieking voices were silenced, then a group of Jewish religious leader's approach Jesus seeking justification for His actions.

"What miraculous sign[31] you show us to prove your authority to do all this?" (John 2:18b NIV)

I wanted to come to the defense of Jesus and share with them that Jesus had just shown us a sign by turning water into wine but Jesus did not need my help in validating His actions to those whose only interest lay in preserving their immoral economic profit. If their request was genuine they could have turned to the sign of the written word of the prophet Malachi who over 450 years earlier wrote, "'Behold, I send my messenger, And He will prepare the way before Me. And the LORD, whom you seek, will suddenly come to His temple, Even the Messenger of the covenant. In whom you delight. Behold, He is coming,' Says the LORD of hosts. 'But who can endure the day of His coming? And who can stand when He appears? For He is like a refiner's fire and like launderers' soap. He will sit as a refiner and a purifier of silver; He will purify the sons of Levi, and purge them as gold and silver, that they may offer to the LORD an offering in righteousness.'" (Malachi 3:1-3 NKJV) For the fulfillment of Scripture was a sign, but those benefitting from the exchange of money such as the sons of Annas were not interested in fulfillment of Scripture, but rather the immoral filling of their pockets. Therefore, they demanded from Jesus a sign that they would find acceptable.

Jesus did not respond like a "supernatural puppet" striving to validate Himself to those whose only interest was self-perseveration of their own power and authority. Instead, Jesus answered them, "Destroy this temple, and in three days I will raise it up" (John 2:19 ESV).

Appalled, the religious leaders looked at each other with jaws dropped and heads shaking before looking back at Jesus and responding, "It has taken forty-six years to build this temple, and You will raise it up in three days?" (John 2:20b)[32]

Papias then asked, "Apostle, it really took 46 years to build The Temple that was started during the rule of Herod?" "The major building occurred in the first ten years and at the time of the first cleansing of the Temple it had taken 46 years just up to that point. Work on the Temple would continue for another 37 years. Then the rebellion of the Jews led to the destruction of The Temple just six years later." "So 83 years to build and it was destroyed six years later"[33] Papias stated in a manner of disbelief.

"Yes my son, remember our hope is not in a building but rather our resurrected LORD.[34] Jesus was not describing The Temple being rebuilt but rather his own body being resurrected from the dead. These words of Jesus will come to fruition three years after Jesus' prophetically stated them.

Jesus cleansing the Temple is symbolic of a command of God in the Law of Moses regarding mildew in someone's home (Leviticus 14:33-55). If someone goes into their home and sees what appears to be mildew or mold, then they are to call a priest to examine. If the priest confirms that substance is mold they need to go through a cleansing process to purify the home. If the mildew returns, then the priest is to condemn the home and it must be destroyed (Leviticus 14:43-45) In order to purify a home that has not been contaminated, there is to be an animal sacrifice involving wood and scarlet yarn (Leviticus 14:51). When Jesus returns in three years He will find the Temple contaminated with the money changers once again. Jesus will be the blood sacrifice involving the wood of the cross and a scarlet robe (Matthew 27:27-28).

"That's amazing!" stated Polycarp in profound awe. "This can't be coincidence, right Apostle?"

The elderly apostle reassuringly stated, "When it comes to the Word of God, there are no coincidences. Only profound truths revealed from Him who knows the end from the beginning. Jesus was foretelling what was to come and in three years when Peter and I would look into an empty tomb this prophetic statement would have come to pass."

Annas and his sons weren't motivated by their calling as priests or obedience to the Scriptures but instead the Temple courtyard was an opportunity for them to increase their wealth and the actions of Jesus subsequently had a negative impact on their economic revenue. Irate, they demanded that Jesus show them a sign that validated His actions in the courtyard. They were livid that Jesus would use a whip to empty the courtyard and while Jesus didn't use the whip to inflict any bodily harm, in a few years, right before He would be crucified whips were used on Jesus with very different intentions. If they wanted a sign they should have seen that the actions of Jesus that day was the fulfillment of a prophecy over 450 years old.

Malachi prophesied, "'Behold, I send my messenger, and he will prepare the way before me. And the LORD whom you seek will suddenly come to His temple; and the messenger of the covenant in whom you delight, behold, He is coming,' says the LORD of hosts" (Malachi 3:1 ESV). The LORD had arrived and cleansed the temple (Malachi 3:3), but He was not recognized by His own people.

After the conclusion of the events at the temple we remained in Jerusalem. While the religious leaders demanded a sign Jesus would not give a sign in an attempt to appease them. Jesus gave many signs to those in Jerusalem whose hearts was more open to the truth and consequently many believed in Jesus. Yet, for all who believed in Jesus this did not signify their level of commitment was complete. Believing in Jesus is one thing but to become a follower is something else entirely. Jesus personally didn't trust them at this time because He knew the heart of man (John 2:24-25)

Chapter 5 Footnotes

[1] In Scripture there are two different Bethany's. One Bethany is where Mary, Martha and Lazarus lived. This Bethany was less than two miles from Jerusalem (John 11:18). The other Bethany is the location of John the Baptist's public ministry. Most scholars place this location in Perea on the east bank of the Jordan River about 23 miles from Jerusalem. [B] Some scholars have argued for a different location. such as Raine Riesner (1987) who states this location actually should be Batanea which is considerably north of the location where most scholars accept. [C]

[2] John 1:38 says, "They said" in reference to when Jesus was asked where he was staying. Scripture doesn't specify that it was John who asked the question. Perhaps they looked at each other and agreed upon the question and one of them asked. My logic for having the Apostle John ask the question is because throughout the Gospel of John, the author goes out of his way to not mention himself by name. In John 1 we see that Andrew, Philip, and Nathaniel are all specifically quoted but John never quotes

himself. So perhaps it was John who asked the question but he puts "they" so as not to credit himself.

3 In John 1:41 we read that "the first thing Andrew did." The transliteration for this Greek adverb is *proton* which means "first, in the first place." Interestingly *protos* means "first in time, place or order of importance." So Andrew's action can have a duel meeting in that getting his brother was the first thing that he did but it was also first in order of importance for things that he needed to do. (biblehub.com)

4 Up to this point Andrew's brother was identified as, "Simon, son of Jonah." Jonah in Aramaic means "John", and "Cephas" means "rock" in Aramaic, and is translated to Peter in Greek. G Translation of Peter isn't just meaning a normal rock that one might find on the ground, but rather a large mass of rock that is taken from the bed-rock, so it is a rock of substance. H

5 We know that Philip was from Bethsaida (John 1:44) and he along with Andrew were probably the two unnamed disciples in John 21:2 as Andrew was always with Peter and Philip with Nathaniel. Philip was a Greek name so he was quite possibly a Hellenistic Jew. I Alexander the Greats Empire stretched in the west from Greece to Egypt in the South and India in the east. This spread Greek culture and brought about the Hellenistic Age. Alexander the Greats father was Philip II of Macedonia so we can see even from this example that Philip is a Greek name, not a Hebrew name. Hellenization is the blending of cultures in the era after Alexander the Great which blended Greek, Hebrew, Persian, Egyptian, and Indian cultures with a heavy Greek education and influence. J

6 Near the end of the Gospel of John we see that Nathaniel is from Cana (John 21:2)

7 We don't know what the conversation with Jesus, and Peter, Andrew, Philip and John was centered around. Perhaps Jesus gave Philip the invitation to invite his friend Nathaniel but we will see later on in the chapter that Jesus already had supernatural knowledge about Nathaniel. By the time Philip arrived to see Nathaniel we know that he was already convinced that Jesus was the fulfillment of prophecy

8 Bethsaida was built by Herod the Great and its population had become predominantly Gentile K Perhaps Nathaniel, someone so focused on the Hebrew Scriptures might have thought that the Gentiles influenced the rational of the early followers of Jesus. This is speculation but certainly viable.

9 Mark 1:21 and 29 combined clearly state that Peter and Andrew were living in Capernaum, yet John 1:44 states that Peter and Andrew were from Bethsaida. This does not show an error in the Scriptures but rather leaves us with two possibilities. One is that Peter and Andrew had two

homes, one in Bethsaida one in Capernaum. The second and I believe more likely scenario is that Peter and Andrew used to live in Bethsaida and then moved to Capernaum. Just like Jesus was known as "Jesus of Nazareth" despite the fact that he didn't live there anymore he was originally from Nazareth and that's why he was referred in this manner and that is what John could be implying in his Gospel writing.

[10] *Alethos* is the adverb used here and it means "truly." The KJV uses the world "indeed." Jesus was not describing Nathaniel's lineage but rather is emphasizing his character and does again when He uses the Greek noun *dolos* stating that there was no "deceit" or "treachery" in him. (biblehub.com)

[11] The fig tree was special to the Jewish people being symbolic of the Temple and Judaism. [L] Additionally, in the Old Testament having fig trees was a sign of prosperity (I Kings 4:25; Micah 4:4; Zechariah 3:10).

[12] This is the first of 25 different occasions in the Gospel of John which Jesus begins a statement by saying, "Truly, truly I say unto you" or "Verily, verily I say unto you." Literally this is "AMEN, AMEN" [M]

[13] Archaeologically two different possible locations for Cana have emerged. One excavation site is referred to as Khirbet Kana (ruins of Cana) [P] and it is the farther north location of the two possibilities (8-9 miles). The other site is a modern village called Kefr Cana (Arabic for village of Cana) and a Roman Catholic Church and Greek Orthodox Church are presently in this village. This village is significantly closer to Nazareth (4-5 miles away). Both options present the reality that Cana and Nazareth were geographically close to each other.

[4] Only in the Gospel of John is the name Nathaniel used. It seems that Nathaniel and Bartholomew are the same person. In each of the synoptic Gospels Philip and Bartholomew are paired together (Matthew 10:3; Mark 3:18; Luke 6:14). How the disciples are paired and grouped together isn't random as James and John were paired with each other every time and Peter and Andrew was always the other two mentioned in the first four. So Philip and Nathaniel's pre-existing bond carried over into how they were paired after following Jesus and this is strong evidence that Nathaniel and Bartholomew are the same person. Additionally, Bartholomew isn't a proper name as translated this name is *bar Tholomais* which means "son of Talmai." [Q]

[15] Wedding celebrations could last as long as a week. [S]

[16] While we don't know who exactly the wedding was for we can rationalize several factors. For starters, Mary the mother of Jesus seemed to have a prominent role at the wedding. She was informed that they were out of wine (John 2:3) and she instructed the servants to do whatever Jesus tells them to do (John 2:4). This would suggest this wedding involved a family member or a close family friend. The relation

presumably would be with the groom since it was his responsibility to pay for the wedding. [T] The reason it doesn't seem like the wedding is from Mary's side of the family is because if it was presumably the Apostle John's family would have been there as well since his mother Salome is the sister of Mary. If they were there then John chose not to mention anyone but if James was there perhaps he would have been compelled to join Jesus and the five followers but there is no indication that this occurred. While some of this can be viewed as speculation there certainly appears to be some merit.

[17] Wedding celebrations varied in duration according to what the family of the groom could afford. They could last anywhere from a day to an entire week

[18] The wine that would have served at the wedding was diluted to be two parts wine to three parts water. [V] This allowed people to not get sick from drinking any impurities that would have been in the water but it was also diluted enough so that drunkenness wouldn't occur.

[19] Some people upon initially reading this passage think the response of Jesus is disrespectful. In our western modern culture, it would definitely be wise for a son not to call his mother "woman." However, in the eastern culture that Jesus was part of this was a respectful response, like calling a woman "Ma'am" or "Madam." [W] For context this is the same word (guné) and address Jesus states while speaking to his mother Mary and the Apostle John while on the cross (John 19:26b- "Woman, behold your son." ESV)

[20] This question can be viewed as Jesus requesting to be left out of this matter.

[21] In the Gospel of John this is the first of five occasions that Jesus declares that His "hour" (hóra) or "time" (kairos) which can also be described as "season" had not yet come (2:4, 7:6, 7:8, 7:30, 8:20) During the Passion Week of Jesus which is the events from the Triumphal Entry through the death and Resurrection, three times in the Gospel of John it is recorded that Jesus mentions that "His hour" or "time" had come (12:23, 13:1, 17:1). So in all eight times Jesus describes His "hour" of "time." During the wedding at Cana, for the first of the "signs" in the Gospel of John is the first time that his "hour" is mentioned.

[22] Obviously we have no way of knowing what side conversations were taking place at this time but it's interesting that in John's account of the feeding of the five thousand that prior to the miracle Jesus asked Philip where they could buy bread for the people to eat. Philip was one of the five disciples at both the changing of the water to wine as well as the feeding of the five thousand but when Jesus asked Philip about buying bread Philip's response wasn't to be reminded of the supernatural act he

witnessed when Jesus turned water into wine but instead focused on the limited natural resources they had at their disposal (John 6:5-7)

[23] Here the Greek noun used for servants is *diakonos* is used by the Apostle Paul two times in I Timothy used to describe deacons (3:8, 3:12) These servants at the wedding were obedient to the will and commands of Jesus. Deacons in the church, who are also servants, are called to do the same thing.

[24] For skeptics who don't believe that the Apostle John is the author of the Gospel of John, this is one of the instances in the Gospels which depict the account of an eyewitness. Recalling how many stone jars was present and their size is descriptive of someone who was present.

[25] In describing Jesus as creator the Apostle Paul States-Colossians 1:16- "For by Him all things were created, in heaven and on earth, visible and invisible, whether thrones or powers or rulers or authorities; all things have been created through Him and for Him." (ESV)

[26] Matthew 13:55- "Isn't this the carpenter's son? Isn't His mother's name Mary, and aren't His brothers named James, Joseph, Simon and Judas?" (NIV)

[27] Romans 10:4- "For Christ is the end of the law for righteousness to everyone who believes." (ESV)

[28] John 2:13 describes that Jesus and his disciples went "up to Jerusalem." Geographically Jerusalem is south of Galilee so the description of "up" isn't based on geographic location but rather elevation. Jerusalem is 2,610 feet above sea level. [BB] So in order to reach that elevation you had to travel "up."

[29] Also spelled Ananus

[30] Jewish writings never refer to this area as the "Court of the Gentiles", instead it is referred to as the "mountain of the house." [FF]

[31] Here the Greek noun for "sign" is *semeion* and it means, "sign, miracle, an indication." This is a request that we will see made by the Pharisees and Sadducees many times during the ministry of Jesus (Matthew 12:38; 16:1; Mark 8:11; Luke 11:16; John 2:18)(www.biblehub.com) This word is used 77 times in the New Testament including 17 times in the Gospel of John.

[32] This verse gives us a timeline for the ministry of Jesus. Josephus stated in the eighteenth year of Herod's reign he "undertook a very great work, that is, to build himself the temple of God." [HH] There is one of two ways to take this dating. The first is when Herod was appointed by the Romans and the second is three years later at the conquest of Jerusalem. The proper dating is referring to the conquest of Jerusalem [II] which was in 37 A.D. which makes the eighteenth year of his reign 19 B.C. If we add the forty-six years that it had taken to build the Temple this would bring us to 27 A.D. when the cleansing of the Temple occurred. So in the events of

John 2 they are 46 years into the building of The Temple but it is not a finished product

[33] Major reconstruction of the Temple lasted about a decade from 19 B.C. to 9 B.C. but work on the Temple continued all the way until 64 A.D. This means that it took 83 to build The Temple and it was destroyed only six years later.

[34] I Peter 1:3- "Blessed be the God and Father of our Lord Jesus Christ! According to His great mercy He has given us new birth into a living hope through the resurrection of Jesus Christ from the dead." (ESV)

Chapter 6

Jerusalem's finest meets Heaven's finest

Jesus speaks to Nicodemus-John 3:1-21

While many individuals of the lower socioeconomic class were drawn to Jesus, a majority of the aristocratic elite wanted nothing to do with Him. There were exceptions, but none who had a higher standing than Nicodemus. Few men in Jerusalem would be considered his equal. Politically, he was one of the 70 members of the Sanhedrin whose influence among the Jewish people spread beyond Judea, and their rulings were to be respected throughout the Roman world when it pertained to matters of the Hebrew people. As a Pharisee in the Sanhedrin Nicodemus was in the minority, since a vast majority of the 70 members were Sadducees. [A] Rarer still, he was all of the aforementioned, but he was also intrigued by Jesus rather than considering him an adversary. Economically, he was a land owner whose fortune was enhanced by renting out his farm to individuals and retaining a portion of the crops.[1] [B] His wealth and power alone were more than enough to place Nicodemus at an exalted position amongst the Jews in Jerusalem. In addition, he was considered the preeminent teacher among the Hebrew people. [C]

Personally, I was surprised when Nicodemus made his way to my father's home in Jerusalem, and, after coming inside and seeing Jesus, humbly addressed Him as "Rabbi." Unquestionably, Jesus was pleased at his arrival but didn't seem surprised that he had come. After everyone had exchanged pleasantries, Nicodemus took on an unfamiliar role. For the first time in probably many years, he had come to be taught rather than to teach.

"Bishop, you had mentioned on a prior occasion that Nicodemus had come at night. Was there any specific reason that this was the time he had chosen to meet with Jesus?" asked Papias.

"Great question my child. The reality is, there are multiple reasons for Nicodemus coming in the evening. Rabbis taught that the best time to study the law was at night so there would be fewer distractions. [D] Certainly, Nicodemus had a reputation to uphold, and being under the cover of darkness also decreased the likelihood of being recognized going into the home where Jesus was staying, so perhaps this was motivation as well." While Nicodemus was not yet openly claiming to be a follower of Jesus, eventually that time would come.[2]

After settling into their respective seats, the five of us were permitted to listen to the conversation between the exalted Jewish ruler and the intriguing Nazarene carpenter.

"Rabbi, we know that you are a teacher come from God, for no one can do these signs that you do unless God is with him" (John 3:2 ESV) said Nicodemus. While a majority of the rulers of the synagogue were incensed by the miraculous works of Jesus, Nicodemus again was in the minority, this time being enamored by the signs of Jesus, but also revealing he was not alone in his assessment. Based on the manner in which he phrased the preceding statement, it is reasonable to presume that Nicodemus expected Jesus to further elaborate on His own purpose for ministry, [E] but Jesus instead centered the conversation on the spiritual needs of Nicodemus. Jesus was the master at not just listening to the question that was asked but, more profoundly, analyzing the heart of the individual asking the question. Jesus chose not to answer the question asked, instead answering the question that should have been asked and sharing truth that needed to be heard.

"Verily, verily", [3] stated Jesus, as He leaned forward stressing the importance of His impending statement. "I say unto thee, except a man be born again [4], he cannot see the Kingdom of God" (John 3:3b KJV). [5] Nicodemus sat up in his chair, put his hand on his chin, and thought for a moment before responding. Nicodemus expected Jesus to have been flattered by his statement that he was a prophet sent by God, similar to Moses (Exodus 3:12), Isaiah (Isaiah 6:9) and Jeremiah (Jeremiah 1:19). Nicodemus instead heard Jesus describe what could be interpreted as a physical impossibility. As a man of wealth and influence, Nicodemus was used to accomplishing that which is practical by use of his resources. Religiously, Nicodemus found justification by strict adherence to the Law of Moses. Perplexed at the physical impossibility of this statement, and perhaps attempting to arrive at the symbolic truth being presented by Jesus, Nicodemus proceeded to ask Jesus how someone could enter their mother's womb for a second time.

Jesus looked at Nicodemus as if to imply that a true student of the word of God, let alone a teacher, should be able grasp the content which Jesus was discussing with Nicodemus. For the second time in their brief discussion Jesus accentuated the significance of the message by stating, "Truly, truly I say to you, unless one is born of water and the Spirit, he cannot enter the Kingdom of God" (John 3:5 ESV). Jesus proceeded to stress that everyone is born of flesh, but, to enter the Kingdom of God, you need to be born of the Spirit. Eternal life comes when we are born from above. Nicodemus was stuck on the concept that good works and adherence to a set of laws was sufficient to enter the Kingdom of God. Another valuable lesson Nicodemus needed to grasp was that Scripture needs to supersede our circumstances. If we were to go back 600 years prior to the conversation that was occurring between Jesus and Nicodemus, we would see that the lesson Jesus was teaching had precedence in the writings of the prophet Ezekiel.[6]

Ezekiel could have focused on the fact that he was supposed to be serving as a priest (Ezekiel 1:3). Living in exile in Babylon, over 500 miles away from Jerusalem, [H] made that impossible. While Ezekiel was in exile in Babylon, the Babylonian army destroyed the Temple. However, God did not leave this displaced prophet without Hope as he was taught a timeless and eternal lesson. Salvation is a work of God not of man. God declared to Ezekiel that He would give him a new heart. He would give Ezekiel a new spirit, and He would put His Spirit in him, and, as a result, Ezekiel would follow the decrees of the LORD (Ezekiel 36:26-27). Yet 600 years later, in my father's house he used for business transactions, one of the most powerful and respected men in all of the Holy City of Jerusalem was struggling with this concept. While in exile, Ezekiel understood that salvation comes from the LORD, while in the stomach of a great fish,

Jonah understood that salvation comes from the LORD (Jonah 2:9), but while thriving in prestige and power Nicodemus was failing to grasp this truth. Nicodemus expected to see the Kingdom of God but couldn't grasp being "born anew." [1]

Nicodemus should have at some point, while being taught by Jesus, connected this passage of Scripture (Ezekiel 36:25-27), but he was too focused on adherence to the law. In order to teach Nicodemus this concept, Jesus used an illustration from a man who predated Ezekiel and Jonah, and the recipient of the Law; this man was Moses. When the children of Israel travelled from Mount Hor around Mount Edom, they sinned against the LORD by angrily speaking against God and Moses. (Numbers 21:4-9). As a result, judgment came in the form of poisonous snakes. When the children of Israel confessed their sins to Moses and asked for deliverance, God instructed Moses to make a bronze snake and put it on a pole. All who looked upon the snake were delivered from death.

"By using this historical example, Jesus was giving a foreshadowing of his own death, right Apostle?" asked Polycarp.

"You are correct my son" came his reply.

"For the children of Israel, snakes became the problem which led to death and looking upon a raised up snake became the solution. Now, the problem with man is man, because man has sinned, and this leads to death.

"For the wages of sin is death" (Romans 6:23a NIV) recited Polycarp.

"Precisely", stated John, "so the solution became God becoming man and Jesus being the man that was raised up so that all who look to Him are saved. When the priest offered a sacrifice he needed to go up steps to the brazen altar (Leviticus 9:22) so each sacrifice was at an elevated place.[7] So the sacrifice was lifted up, and the bronze serpent was lifted up; and they are a foreshadowing of Jesus, and He needs to be lifted up," affirmed the aged Apostle.

"Amazing how much of the Scriptures point towards Jesus," stated Papias.

"True my son! 'For in perfect faithfulness you have done marvelous things, things planned long ago,'" (Isaiah 25:1b NIV) stated the Apostle, as he quoted from Isaiah.

"Do you think that Nicodemus could have envisioned that Jesus was describing His own death?" asked Polycarp.

"No my son; Nicodemus was wealthy and powerful, and, along with the other Pharisees who were eagerly anticipating the arrival of the Messiah, expected to witness majesty and splendor, not degradation and shame." ᴸ "

This was a stumbling block for many Pharisees, right Apostle?" spoke Papias.

"For certain it was. In time, this would not be a stumbling block for Nicodemus, as the truth would be revealed to him, along with another former Pharisee who recognized that Jesus became our sin so we could become 'the righteousness of God' (II Corinthians 5:21), and of course I am talking about the Apostle Paul."

Part of Nicodemus' problem is that he had expectations of what he wanted Jesus to say. Jesus wasn't intrigued by the expectations of Nicodemus; His concern was what Nicodemus needed to hear instead of what he wanted to hear. Nicodemus expected to hear about God as judge and the Messiah exalted in glory. Instead, Jesus shared about the love of God and the Messiah exalted as a result of our shame. For the purpose of the ministry of Jesus, the salvation message can be summed up with these words: "For God so loved[8] the world, that He gave His only begotten[9] Son, that whosoever believeth in Him, shall not perish but have eternal life" (John

3:16 KJV). Nicodemus was filled with knowledge but Jesus was teaching "Israel's teacher" this was not sufficient, for Scripture pointed towards Jesus as the Messiah, and it was vital for Nicodemus to believe[10] in this truth."

"As seen by the ministry of John the Baptist and other prophets, when sharing of the Blessings that come from above, there is also a warning for those who reject the message. Jesus is the light of the world, and the main reason for the hatred against Jesus is that His light was exposing the darkness by which so many were living. When Nicodemus left that evening, I don't believe he heard what he expected, but Jesus gave him what he needed to hear. Nicodemus would eventually come to another realization, which was to follow Jesus he would have to abandon the lofty status of which so many placed him. Nicodemus exited in the same quiet manner in which he arrived, but the flaws in how he was living were now uncovered after his encounter with the light of the world, Jesus Christ.

Jesus Exalted by His Forerunner

John 3:22-36

Since becoming followers of Jesus in a short period of time, we travelled together to Cana then to Capernaum and then

Jerusalem. After our time in Jerusalem was complete, Peter shared the sentiments of the five of us when he asked, "Are we going back to Capernaum?" We were all more comfortable being around fellow Galileans than continuing to be among Judeans, particularly those from Jerusalem for an extended period of time.

"Not yet," stated Jesus.

We all felt a touch of disappointment as were ready to be amongst our own people. We travelled eastward, through the Judean wilderness and then began to travel north. Andrew and I looked at each other to communicate without using words. Were we going to see John the Baptist? Would he and his followers now join us as well? Time would tell, but this much is true, I had continually attempted to guesstimate what would occur next, and I had yet to be right. This trend would continue.

Our destination would be a place known as Aenon, which was in the Jordan Valley, slightly west of the Jordan River. This was substantially north of where we were with John the Baptist, but his ministry at this time was not confined to one place. Instead, he traveled up and down the Jordan River ministering and serving the Kingdom of God.[110] So we were now in the vicinity of where John the Baptist was furthering his ministry, but Jesus intentionally stopped short of unifying the two groups. Much of the ministry of Jesus was located around water, and this next short phase would be no different, as we were by a spring of water. Shortly after our arrival, a few more made their way towards our direction. The five of us were unsure what we were doing there, and of our responsibilities, so naturally we just stood there and looked at each other, seemingly more effective than the proverbial sticking a foot in our mouths, as we would become famous for doing. As the people travelled closer, Jesus stepped into the forefront and began preaching a message of repentance and baptism. This was a topic that I had heard before. [12] As he preached the crowd continued to grow, and then he offered an invitation. This message was heartily received and a line began to form of individuals receiving the invitation to be baptized.

"Look familiar?" Andrew said to me leaning over with a smile, expressing the similarities that we had seen before.

"Yes it does" I replied, "and once again we will have the best view."

Once again, my presumption was wrong. Andrew and I expected to watch Jesus as we had watched John the Baptist baptize countless individuals. Instead of walking into the stream of water, Jesus walked over toward the five of us and gave us this command, "baptize them."

This seemed like the responsibility of John the Baptist or Jesus, not a young fisherman like me. Peter wasn't as hesitant; as we will see, there were multiple times he would be the first of us in the water. Suddenly, the relatively remote location of Aenon was receiving great amounts of attention. One day, I looked out and noticed some familiar faces that I had seen before, as they were disciples of John the Baptist. Curiosity brought them to Aenon but they left perhaps more confused as they didn't come to be baptized. Curiosity brought them there and they were certainly taken back at the sight of Andrew and I along with the other three all baptizing others.[13]

Personally these were men that I knew, and I can speak to their passion and dedication. They sacrificed to be a disciple of John the Baptist and now questions were arising in their minds. Jesus, a man whom John the Baptist baptized, was having people flock to hear him as his disciples, some of whom were disciples of John the Baptist, and they were baptizing others. Now, Jewish religious leaders were verbally attacking the ministry of John the Baptist. After all, the Jewish law had its own systems of purifications and washings, what was the need for this wilderness prophet's teaching of baptism?

These men responded in a wise manner by bringing their questions to John the Baptist rather than try to figure out the answers amongst themselves. While followers of John the Baptist were annoyed at the attention Jesus was receiving, John's support of Jesus receiving more attention was consistent with his ministry. Q Prophets of God often speak in similar metaphors, and just like Isaiah (54:5-6; 62:5), Jeremiah (2:2), and Hosea (2:19-20) before him, John the Baptist used wedding and marital imagery to unveil the relevancy of his ministry and how God was working through him. John continued the standard that he set from the start of his ministry, which was to point towards the true Messiah, the Christ and he personally was not that man (John 1:20; 3:28). If the Messiah was to be viewed as the groom in a wedding, John the Baptist viewed himself as the friend of the groom.[14] John the Baptist was there to "support the groom", "support the Christ," but John himself was not that man. Just as the groom is to receive the attention at a wedding rather than a groomsman, so the Christ was to receive this attention, not His forerunner. For to John the Baptist, the true purpose of his ministry was for the ministry of Jesus to grow, His influence to grow, and His impact to become greater. John the Baptist recognized that true success of his ministry was when the ministry of Jesus Christ far surpassed his own. Of all the things that John the Baptist was, his origins were of this world and his eternity would be in heaven, thanks to the work of the Messiah. Jesus Christ was the only man who was sent from heaven, and through Him our eternity in heaven will become secure. pertaining to his own. The ministry is summed up best by using his own words when talking about Jesus, "He must become greater; I must become less" (John 3:30 NIV). [15]

Chapter 6 Footnotes

[1] While Scripture does not specify this is how Nicodemus obtained his wealth this was common among the aristocratic members of the Sanhedrin

[2] In the Gospel of John, it specifies that Nicodemus came at night but it doesn't elaborate as to why. Many scholars have reasoned that Nicodemus didn't want it to be known that he visited Jesus. This certainly could be one of if not the reason Nicodemus arrived at night. Considering all Nicodemus had going on it could be reasoned that this was when Nicodemus was free so he sought out Jesus at a time in which he would be uninterrupted. This also ties into the Rabbinical way of thinking that nighttime would naturally have less distractions. What we can certainly rationale is that Nicodemus was a witness to multiple miraculous works by Jesus prior their discussion (John 3:2), in the future Nicodemus would become more vocal against how Jesus was being viewed by the religious leaders (John 7:50-51) and lastly his public action with Joseph of Arimathea in burying Jesus after His death leaves no doubt where they stood in being a follower if Jesus. While the Gospel of John does describe Joseph of Arimathea as secretly being a disciple over "fear of the Jews" (John 19:38) Nicodemus was never described in this manner.

[3] The word "verily" which can also be translated "truly" was used twice to implore Nicodemus to be fully engaged because what Jesus was going to say was of great importance. [F] This will be used again just two verses later in John 3:5

[4] Here the adverb for the word often translated "again" is *anothen* and a better translation would actually be, "from above" as "ano" means from above so "born from above" is more accurate than "born again." Other instances that this word is used (John 19:11, James 1:17)

[5] This verse describes the spiritual act of regeneration. Nicodemus was confused thinking Jesus was describing a physical act by man but regeneration is a spiritual action performed by God. Regeneration is described as, "the act of God, the Holy Spirit whereby in response to salvational faith He imparts spiritual life to the Gospel believer." [G] Regeneration is done on our behalf by God (John 1:13, Colossians 2:13, I John 5:1;4) with work specifically done by God the Father (I Peter 1:3), God the Son (John 10:28), and God the Holy Spirit (Galatians 5:25, Titus 3:5)

[6] Ezekiel and Daniel were both prophets used by God while in exile in Babylon. Daniel was part of the first group of exiles in 605 B.C. and Ezekiel was part of the second group of exiles in 597 B.C. The book of Ezekiel is written starting in 592 B.C. and ends in 571 B.C. [J]

[7] Altar means, "high place." [K]

[8] This word for love is *agapao* which means, "I love, wish well to, take pleasure in, long for; denotes the love of reason, esteem" (biblehub.com) This verb is used 143 times in the New Testament including three times in the chapter of John 3 (16, 19, 35). One verse which *agapao* or *agape* is used three times and profoundly expresses the love of God the Father and God the Son is John 15:9- "As the Father has loved me, so have I loved you. Now remain in my love." (NIV)

[9] This adjective that is used is *monogenes* and means, "only" or "unique" (biblehub.com). Scholars have connected the similarities of the sacrifice of Jesus to Abraham sacrificing his son (Genesis 22:1-4).[M] When God tells Abraham to take "your only son, Isaac" (Genesis 22:2) Isaac was the only son that Abraham had with Sarah, but he had another son, Ishmael. In fact, the author of Hebrews uses *monogenes* to describe Isaac as the "one and only" or "unique" son of Abraham (Hebrews 11:17). So Isaac was "unique" to Abraham in that he was the Covenantal Son of promise, the and Jesus was "unique" to God the Father in that He is the Son who is also part of the Trinity, and with whom the New Covenant would be established. *Monogenes* is used nine times in the New Testament but only by three authors: Luke, John, and the author of Hebrews. Some of the passages of Scriptures include describing the only son of a widow (Luke

7:12), the relationship of God the Father and God the Son (John 3:16, 18) and the relationship of Abraham and Isaac (Hebrews 11:17)

[10] The Greek verb repeatedly used by John is *pisteuo* which means, "believe, entrust, have faith in" (biblehub.com). This word appears 98 times in the Gospel of John [N] and seven times from John 3:11-21 alone.

[11] The exact location of Aenon and Salim are debated primarily between two different locations. They don't appear to be close to the original location where Jesus was baptized. Aenon was substantially north of that location. Both of these locations were geographically in Judea but close to Samaria. Aenon in Arabic means "many waters" or "many springs" and each potential location has plenty of water. [P] Many scholars make the strong case that by this time John the Baptist would minister in different location up and down the Jordan Valley and this appears to be true

[12] In this narrative the Apostle John does not claim that Jesus was preaching prior to anyone becoming baptized but naturally we can presume that this was the case. We wouldn't expect anyone to naturally walk up to them and ask to be baptized. John the Baptist would preach and he was the forerunner for Jesus so it makes sense that Jesus would preach, and as John 4:2 specifies the disciples would be the ones who would do the baptizing

[13] John doesn't specify that disciples of John the Baptist witnessed the baptisms that occurred at Aenon by the disciples of Jesus but they did know about them and they questioned this activity to him

[14] We would view that as the "best man"

[15] This quote by John the Baptist is his last recorded as part of his ministry prior to his imprisonment. [R] John 3:31-36 is part of the narrative but does not appear to be a direct quote by John the Baptist. The Message in these verses are consistent with the ministry of John the Baptist

Chapter 7

Act of Restoration at a well

John 4:1-39

Once Jesus committed the holy act of cleansing the Temple he would be under continual scrutiny, especially while in Judea. Upon hearing that the baptismal ministry of Jesus had eclipsed the ministry of John the Baptist, the Pharisees sought to drive a wedge between the two. [A] Simply put, debates on baptism and purification rituals intensified, [B] and it became more productive to move onward and impact different lives than remain stagnant in an increasingly stifling environment. So despite being nowhere near Jerusalem, Jesus thought it best to leave Judea altogether.

As we prepared to leave and head back to Galilee, Jesus let it be known we would take the most direct route, which meant travelling through Samaria. One similarity between Judeans and Galileans was the disdain that each had for the Samaritans; where they differed was the degree of contempt shown. Travelling through Samaria for the Galilean was not the preferred route but one which was made at times due to its convenience; however, a Pharisee from Judea would choose to go up the eastern side of the Jordan River through Perea to avoid Samaria altogether.[1] [C]

"As you know my sons, the unified nation of Israel was split in two after the death of Solomon and during the reign of his son Rehoboam.[2] For nearly two centuries, they ruled as two separate nations, the northern nation of Israel and the southern nation of Judah, which was significantly smaller in land mass but had the prestige of Jerusalem and the Temple built by Solomon. During this time, a new, terrifying empire emerged known as the Assyrians. On the battlefield, they would conquer their opponent through power, speed, and precision, equipped with a large army and deadly chariots, each armed with three men: a driver, archer, and shield bearer. [D] Perhaps most intimidating about the ancient Assyrians was their method of torture including impaling people, skinning them alive, and carrying off heads as trophies.

"Who would be able to stand up against them?" inquired Polycarp.

"When they were the most powerful empire in the world? Nobody!" answered John. One action the independent nations of Judah and Israel both agreed upon: it was better to for them pay tribute to the Assyrian Empire than to stand up to their military.[3] When someone did finally stand up to them, they paid an extremely heavy price, far more than the tribute they were paying. Approximately 750 years before Jesus and the five of us ventured into Samaria, the last king of Israel was removed from office. Hoshea[4], which ironically means "salvation", sought out the help of Egypt rather than the LORD. This act would ultimately bring an end the kingdom of Israel. Once Hoshea decided to not pay tribute to the Assyrians their leader Shalmaneser V made a siege around Samaria for three years (II Kings 17:5). Prior to the invasion of the Assyrian army, the people of Israel worshipped pagan gods, set up wooden idols, and offered sacrifices to false gods. God sent prophets to the people of the land of Israel imploring them to turn from their wicked ways, but they sought deliverance from the very nation, Egypt, from which God delivered them over 700 years earlier. God gave them what they were asking, removed Himself from their protection, and this became their destruction.

Shalmaneser V, who took over for his father Tiglath-Pileser III, would not be undermined by the refusal of Israel to pay tribute. Within a short period of time, Hoshea was imprisoned, Samaria was conquered, many of its inhabitants were taken away to Mesopotamia and Media, [H] and the Kingdom of Israel was no more. People of different gentile nations were brought into Samaria (II Kings 17:24). These people, who did not know or worship the LORD, intermarried with those who remained. Their children were therefore part Jew and part Gentile, and their descendants became known as the Samaritans.

"Besides the fact that they were considered partial descendants of pagans, were there any other reasons for the hostility between the Jew and Samaritans?" questioned Polycarp.

"Valid question my son. In the eyes of the Jewish people, the actions of the Samaritans revealed them to be opportunists. Consistently, they would try to use their mixed race to their own advantage. If identifying with the Jews benefitted the Samaritans, they would do so; however, if they had nothing personal to gain, they would distance themselves despite having a common lineage."

When Nehemiah obtained permission from King Artaxerxes of Persia to help rebuild Jerusalem after its decimation over 140 years earlier by the Babylonian army, the Samaritans were sought to halt those efforts. Sanballat, the governor of Samaria, was concerned that rebuilding Jerusalem would harmfully impact Samarian trade so the Samaritans joined forces with Arabs, Ammonites, and Ashdodites in resisting the efforts to rebuilt Jerusalem. (Nehemiah 4:1-9).

"So in this instance the Samaritans allied themselves with enemies of the Jews because it didn't benefit them financially" stated Polycarp.

"Yes my son" answered the Apostle John. "In the rare instance when the Jews would find favor with a foreign power, the Samaritans were quick to claim they shared genealogy with the Jews." "Can you give us an example Apostle?" asked Polycarp.

"Well you're asking a lot, but since I am old and have nowhere else to be I guess I can answer your question," joked the Apostle John. "Approximately one century after Nehemiah completed his efforts to rebuild the walls of Jerusalem; an army marched into Jerusalem under the leadership of a man for whose exploits are unmatched historically. This man is Alexander the Great of Macedonia. He was on a quest to conquer the known world and, in doing so, unified peoples on three separate continents under the language of the Greeks. As Alexander approached the city of Jerusalem, he was greeted with elevated standing, and he saluted the high priest. The high priest, along with the other priests, all saluted Alexander with one voice. Alexander then entered Jerusalem and went with the priests to the Temple where a sacrifice was offered to God. The book of Daniel was shown to Alexander, and when they shared that this prophetic book stated one of the Greeks was to destroy the Persian Empire, Alexander believed that he personally was the fulfillment of this prophecy.[5] Alexander treated the Jews very favorably and granted the requests that the priests made to Alexander.[6]

Some Jews joined Alexander as he marched northward to the region of Samaria. After hearing how generous Alexander was towards the Jews, the Samaritans were eager to identify as Jews themselves.

"So are you saying if Alexander the Great had treated the Jews harshly than the Samaritans would have been quick to disassociate with the Jews entirely?" asked Papias.

"Exactly my son," answered the apostle.

"So how did they distinguish themselves as Jewish?" stated Papias.

John answered, "They specified that their genealogy traces back to Abraham through Joseph, the son of Jacob and Ephraim and Manasseh, who were the sons of Joseph." [K]

"Was this true?" asked Papias seeking further clarification.

"Yes, it was true, and in this instance it was a convenient truth. Yet it was also true that they were the product of intermarriage of pagan foreigners who didn't identify with the Hebrews people, their customs, or the worship of

YHWH. The Samaritans continually identified with whichever descendants benefited them in the present circumstances which came across to the Jews as disingenuous and resulted in a deep seated hatred between the Jews and Samaritans that only intensified over the centuries.[7]

"So, while the divide between the Jews and the Samaritans began about 750 years prior to walking through Samaria, the repeated practice of aligning themselves with Jewish enemies, or identifying with the Jews for their own benefit, caused a cultural divide amongst people whom shared geographical borders. This ethnic divide caused a rift, which no leader desired to bridge, between the peoples of who were both descendants of Abraham, Isaac, and Jacob. Nobody, that is, until Jesus. Suddenly, we found ourselves in between the Jordan River and the Mediterranean Sea, south of Galilee but north of Judea; we found ourselves in Samaria.

After travelling a considerable distance, we came to a well. The water would have been tremendously refreshing, if only we had something to draw the water out from the well. With the lateness of the morning, the penetrating heat was intense but not yet reached its climax.

"Why don't we all travel to the town to buy some food before continuing on in our journey?" suggested Nathaniel. Since we were in an area of considerable friction towards Galileans, he thought it best to maximize our minimal numbers. Initially, this appeared to be the wise decision, but nobody had yet noticed that Jesus was exhausted.[8] While Jesus hadn't travelled more than the rest of us, the burden of His ministry was being shown through His fatigue.

Andrew intervened, "Rabbi, why don't you stay here at the well. The five of us can certainly pick up what we need from the town; there is no need for you to come along."

"Besides," Philip answered, "at this time of the morning nobody should be coming to the well for water so you can just stay here and rest." Jesus appreciated the concern He was shown and the five of us were on our way. While I was uncomfortable leaving Jesus behind alone, what I didn't know at the time, but what Jesus knew all along, was that He would not be alone for long.

While I described the religious, cultural, and ethnic divide that occurred as a result of the invasion of the Assyrians, Jews and Samaritans both traced themselves back to the patriarchs Abraham, Isaac, and Jacob. Over 1,900 years' prior, Jacob, a mutual forefather to the Jews and Samaritans bought a plot of ground for 100 pieces of silver (Genesis 33:18-20). After pitching his tent, Jacob built an altar to the LORD and named it *El Elohe Israel* which means, "the mighty God of Israel."[9] Now, nearly two millennia after Jacob and his eleven sons (Benjamin wasn't born yet) rested on this land, Jesus, the Messiah, "the mighty God of Israel," was resting beside a well. Jacob's relationship with his brother Esau was restored on this land and now Jesus was about to restore a woman who understood better than anyone what it felt like to be rejected.

Jesus described to me later the events that occurred after we had left to buy food. About the sixth hour (12:00 noon our time) a woman came to the well to draw water. This was uncharacteristic due to the intense heat of the midday, especially for this time of year. [10] While the five of us never would have expected someone to come, this was the very reason we "had to" go through Samaria. Jesus later shared with us the events so clearly in his masterful art of storytelling that I could picture the conversation as if I were a silent bystander.

My own first impression of the woman when I saw her upon our return was while she appeared to be significantly older than I was at the time but nonetheless, a beautiful woman. [11] Daily, she made this trip when the temperature was most torrid. Each outing yielded the same results: intense heat leading to greater exhaustion while retrieving refreshing water. Worst of all, she was lonely when she left, she was lonely while at the well, and she was lonely when she returned. This time would be different. After walking to the well by herself, she was shocked to see a Galilean sitting there. Since culturally Jews had nothing to Samaritans, the woman was trying to avoid what appeared to be an awkward situation. Her intentions were to retrieve her water and then head back to the village without having to say a word to anyone, just as she had done countless times. Jesus had other intentions.

As she approached the well she gazed directly forward to avoid any eye contact until Jesus simply requested, "Will you give me a drink?" Understandably, Jesus was thirsty and with the Jordan River lying significantly to the east and no tributaries reaching this region the only accessible water was the spring that flowed into Jacob's well.[12]

Startled with receiving a request from a Jew, the woman replied by simply stating the obvious etiquette of that day, she was a Samaritan woman and Jesus was a Jew, so how could He make such a request? Jesus responded that He had something better than the water she could offer; Jesus could offer her "living water."

Confusing the spiritual metaphor, the woman asked, "Sir, you have nothing to draw with and the well is deep. Where do you get this living water?" (John 4:11 NIV) Questioning the logistics of Jesus drawing water was a logical observation, but Jesus was clearly speaking symbolically. There was an abundance of water in the well, thanks to the underground stream, but the depth of 66 feet did not allow for the retrieval of this water without proper resources.[13] After indicating that Jesus was ill-equipped to draw water her next response was more disparaging then genuine.

"Are you greater[14] than our father Jacob? He gave us this well and drank from it himself, as did his sons and his livestock." (John 4:12 ESV)

While her intentions in asking the question was far from authentic, this allowed an avenue for Jesus to further reveal truths of God. Jesus wasn't interested in trading insults with this woman. The village in Samaria which this woman called home saw her merely as an immoral reject. Unworthy of being associated with anybody, she was no longer offered the right hand of fellowship. Jesus, unlike anyone who had ever come into this woman's life, showed compassion and was prepared to offer her Living water not found in the bottom of

Jacob's well. David spoke of a "fountain of life" (Psalm 36:9) as did his son Solomon (Proverbs 13:14). The prophet Jeremiah wrote that by rejecting the LORD the people have rejected "the spring of living water" (Jeremiah 17:13). Zechariah described that from Jerusalem will flow "living water" (Zechariah 14:8).

All of what Jesus was saying up to this point appeared foreign to this woman, which shouldn't be surprising. Samaritans only accepted the first five books of Scripture, which were written by Moses, [S] so they wouldn't have had access to the other books of the Old Testament, including the historical books, books of poetry, and the books of prophecy written by 16 different men.[15] Isaiah stated the invitation of God, "Come, all you who are thirsty, come to the waters" (Isaiah 55:1a). Alongside Jacob's well were two people: A Samaritan woman who was thirsty in ways she failed to comprehend and Jesus, the fulfillment of the words of the prophets who was there to quench her spiritual thirst. While the Samaritan woman showed hesitation to honor the request of Jesus for water from Jacob's well, Jesus willingly shared that the "water" He had to offer springs forth eternal life to the recipient.[16] Suddenly charmed by the conversation and intrigued by what Jesus had to say, she was the one requesting a drink, asking for the living water.

Jesus then made a curious request, "Go, call your husband and come back."

What thoughts must have crossed her mind after hearing this request? Perhaps she felt relief believing that finally she was with someone who didn't know her story. Maybe she felt a little guilty not being sure exactly how to answer the question. Personally, I feel like she saw this as an opportunity. Up until now, the only time anyone viewed her with any value was when she could please a man with her body. Certainly she had no desire to share her past history. She was judged enough for how she lived her life. Maybe this Galilean at the well was looking for something more. She didn't understand about "living water"; satisfying one man at a time until he was done with her was the story of her adult life. So she answered, "I have no husband" and then waited to see if Jesus would respond in the same manner as the men that had come before.

Jesus quickly dismissed that notion by sharing He knew her story: She had taken five husbands and was currently living with a man to whom she wasn't married. Jesus' response rejected her perception that He was similar to the sinful men of her past. Horrified that this man, whom she never encountered prior to the meeting at the well, knew all about her moral failures; all she could think to do was change the subject. No longer would she dismiss His requests, question His resources, or make sarcastic responses to His statements. Here was a man whom she had never met yet knew everything about her. This man appeared to be like a prophet of ancient days. Rather than focus on her actions of the past, her curiosity caused her to ask a question that divided Jewish and Samaritan religious leaders for centuries. Where were they to worship?

Every Passover Jews from Judea, Galilee, and other parts of the world would travel to Jerusalem to commemorate the delivery of their ancestors from bondage. Every Passover the Samaritans, whose descendants were delivered from that same bondage, would travel to Mount Gerizim in Samaria. Before entering the Promised Land, one of the commands of God to His people was to choose a place for the LORD to dwell with them (Deuteronomy 12:5). For the Jews, the place that was set apart for God to dwell with them was Mount Zion, one of the four Mounts on which Jerusalem was built and where the Temple was located. So the Samaritan woman was asking a highly debated question of that day when she inquired, "Where are we to go to worship the LORD, Mount Zion or Mount Gerizim?"

"Apostle" Papias interjected, "Why did the Samaritans choose Mt. Gerizim? Did it hold any historical significance?"

"Moses commanded the children of Israel after they entered into the Promised Land that the tribes of Simeon, Levi, Judah, Issachar, Joseph and Benjamin were to stand on Mount Gerizim to pronounce blessings (Deuteronomy 27:12). Samaritans traced their lineage back to Joseph, and, therefore, were the recipients of the blessings pronounced by Joshua after they had entered the Promised Land (Joshua 8:33). Mt. Gerizim became significant practically as soon as the children of Israel entered into the Promised Land and there was no Mount of greater historical importance in all of Samaria than Gerizim," answered the Apostle.

Since the Samaritans were not going to the Temple in Jerusalem they decided to build their own on Mt. Gerizim centuries earlier.[17]

"Did you ever see the Samaritan Temple?" chimed in Papias. "No my son, approximately 140 years before Jesus and the rest of us met this woman at Jacob's well, the Samaritan Temple at Mount Gerizim was destroyed by an outside force.

"Really?" stated Polycarp, "who destroyed their Temple?"

"Was it the Romans?" reasoned Papias.

"*Teknion* (little/dear children), we have discussed over the centuries how outside armies came into Judea to conquer. When the Samaritan Temple was destroyed, this was an act of conquest by an army coming from Judea.

"The army that invaded Samaria and destroyed the Samaritan Temple were Jewish?" stated Polycarp.

"Yes, for approximately 80 years (143-63 B.C.) Jews independently ruled themselves in Judea. The Seleucid Empire, which was based in Syria, was a continual oppressor and, rather than always be on the defensive," Judea decided to be the aggressor for a change. Approximately 30 years after their independence, John Hyrcannus, who was the high priest, military commander, and civil ruler, led a military force into Samaria and destroyed the Samaritan Temple at Mt. Gerizim."

"Even though the Samaritan Temple was destroyed this didn't stop the people from coming year after year to Mt. Gerizim to celebrate Passover?" asked Papias.

"Not for the last 140 years," answered John.

"They were extremely dedicated then," stated Polycarp in a factual manner.

"Absolutely", John answered, "and by going into Samaria Jesus offered truth in addition to their dedication. Jesus shared that the importance wasn't found in being in Jerusalem on Mount Zion or in Samaria on Gerizim. It's not the mountain that's important, it's the Messiah. Salvation comes from the Jews through the fulfillment of Jewish Scriptures and the Messiah being of the lineage of Abraham and David. The truth of the Message would quickly reach the Samaritans and Gentiles. When Solomon built the Temple, he recognized that the building couldn't contain God (I Kings 8:27). God cannot be confined to a building or a Mountain. God is Spirit (John 4:24) and rather than dwell on the chosen mountain of Jews or Samaritans, the fulfillment of the New Covenant showed that God's Law would be written in their hearts (Jeremiah 31:33).

While this must have been of great encouragement to the woman, Jesus still stressed to her that Salvation is from the Jews.

Polycarp then asked, "Bishop, how would you characterize saying that 'Salvation is of the Jews?"

"Well, my son, for starters Jesus, the Messiah, the source of our salvation is Jewish, with a lineage that traced from Abraham through Isaac, Jacob, Judah and David. Secondly, while the Samaritans rejected the writings of the prophets, these prophetic books, inspired by the Holy Spirit, are part of the Jewish Scriptures, and they foretold of the life and ministry of Jesus centuries prior to His birth. Be certain, salvation is from the Jews, but it is available to everyone."

When this Samaritan woman saw Jesus, she recognized Him to be a Jew. After listening to Him for a short period of time her conclusion was that He must be a prophet. Lastly, Jesus revealed to her that He was the Messiah for whom Jews and Samaritans were waiting and He would guide them into all truth.

Jesus' mission to speak to the Samaritan woman coincided mostly with our "mission" to get food for the six of us, but through God's Divine Providence we didn't miss the entire conversation. When Jesus was around religious leaders, He didn't share that He was the Messiah because their hearts weren't receptive. Right after Jesus' remarkable revelation to the woman, we were returning to the well. As we were walking, we discussed what possibly lay ahead, and we all couldn't wait to get out of Samaria.

Once again Jesus had other plans. When we left Jesus He was tired, hungry, and isolated. Much to our surprise[18], as we approached we saw that at least the last no longer applied.

Was Jesus really speaking to a Samaritan woman while sitting by Jacob's well? We talked among ourselves while at a considerable distance. This was considered inappropriate by the standards of our upbringing, and while we quietly questioned the actions of Jesus out of earshot, none of us dared to verbalize these concerns in His presence. This isn't to say that Jesus didn't know what we were speaking about to each other and what was on our minds. Of course Jesus knew! Rather than justify His actions through a discussion, which Jesus certainly didn't need to do, we were all going to be witnesses to the fruit of His labor.

Understandably the Samaritan woman felt much more comfortable with Jesus than she did when the five of us arrived. So she returned to her village but this time with a true purpose.

"She left her water jar",[19] Philip stated shortly after she had left.

"She will be back" Jesus shared factually.

I remember thinking how she travelled all this way to get water but leaving her jar behind defeated the purpose as to why she came to the well in the first place. What we didn't realize is that she is the reason why Jesus came to the well, and Jesus was the reason she would be returning with people from her village.

Jesus would use the time in-between the woman leaving and returning to the well as a teaching opportunity.

Andrew was the first to speak up, "Rabbi eat something," he encouraged offering Jesus some of the food that we had bought from town. Jesus politely declined stating He didn't want anything to eat.

"Rabbi please" we all encouraged, "have something to eat."

Jesus dismissed our prodding, "I have food that you know nothing about."

Well we certainly didn't know of any such food, and knew He didn't have any food with him when we left Him by the well.

Peter turned to the rest of us and said, "Did someone else bring Jesus food that I don't know about?"

We all shook our heads but what we didn't realize is that Jesus was not talking about the same type of food that we were. Jesus didn't deny our offer to eat because He was no longer hungry. Quite the contrary, but Jesus always chooses the greater good. In this instance, using His hunger as an opportunity to teach us about that which is Spiritual and eternal was greater than appeasing His own hunger pains. As humans, our instinct is to satisfy our need for food, but Jesus put emphasis on the spiritual over the physical. Jesus elaborated on this point by comparing His work to that of farmers. Harvesting crops occur when they are ripe and ready. Evangelizing to souls who are lost allows for them to be "harvested" for the Kingdom of God. Eventually, we would understand this is exactly what Jesus did with the Samaritan woman. As a result, this "harvesting" paid immediate dividends.

Farming and fishing are very different. As fishermen we often received the benefit of immediate dividends for our labor. We get on a boat, cast the net, and catch the fish. Farming requires a completely different discipline in which the farmer doesn't reap the benefit of his labor for months after the work begins. Farmers know based on the time of year and the crops themselves when it is time for harvesting. Jesus knew about the work that had already been completed by many others in preparing the hearts and minds of people to receive the good news that the Messiah had come.

"Who were these people that labored to prepare people to receive the good news of the Gospel?" asked Papias.

The prophet Isaiah served under good kings like Jotham and Hezekiah and bad kings like Ahaz and Manasseh,[20] but regardless of the king of Judah, Isaiah prophesied and labored by foretelling of the coming Messiah, Jesus Christ. Jeremiah labored in the midst of suffering, rejection, and hunger, nearly dying after being tossed into a pit, but he wrote of a new covenant that would be established through Jesus. Daniel and Ezekiel were exiled far away from Jerusalem in Babylon, but they were close to God and faithfully labored by prophesying about Jesus. Many others labored as well until lastly…

"Malachi" interjected Polycarp smiling proudly, presuming he was correct with his interruption. "Malachi was certainly one of the laborers who prophecies pointed towards Jesus but he was not the last. This task belonged to John the Baptist, preaching a message of repentance and preparing hearts and minds for the spiritual harvest when Jesus would emerge on the scene.

While the Samaritan woman was going to her village to bring them to meet show the Messiah, Jesus used this time to teach us through illustrations what it means to reap a "spiritual harvest." Prior to our return to the well, Jesus was "sowing a seed" in the heart and mind of the Samaritan woman which would reap immediate dividends. During His instruction to us, Jesus challenged everyone to "open our eyes" to see the harvest. As Jesus completed His teaching, our eyes saw the Samaritan woman returning to the well with numerous people from her village. They were so captivated by her boldness in sharing about what she experienced that they had to see this man for themselves. As I looked at the people who were approaching, my "eyes" were open to the harvest.

When describing Jesus, the Samaritan woman said, "He told me everything I ever did" (John 4:39). Personally, I am not sure what the people in the village found more impressive: that Jesus told the woman everything that she had done or the fact that despite Jesus knowing her shortcomings He had compassion on her anyway. These villagers were thirsting for more truth and Jesus was there to quench this need. They invited Jesus and the five of us to stay, and we did, for two more days. Earlier, I shared with you that Jesus stated we "had to" go through Samaria and we were puzzled by the necessity. Journeying through Samaria was the quicker route by two days. Perhaps, we thought, Jesus had somewhere He needed to be. Then, we stayed in the Samaritan village for two days and I realized that we "had to" go through Samaria because Jesus "had to" go to Jacob's well, because He "had to" speak to a Samaritan woman, because spiritually, this woman and her village were ripe for the harvest. That is why we "had to." Because Ephraim was still God's dear son, and God remembered him, (Jeremiah 31:20) and because this Samaritan woman was God's dear daughter, and He remembered her. While the Samaritans may have forsaken God and dug their own cisterns, God remembered them. When Jesus came to the well, they experienced the spring of living water (Jeremiah 2:13).

Modern Day Application

Everybody has a story. When the Samaritan woman in John 4 left her village late in the morning to retrieve water from Jacob's well, she was an individual in bondage due to her past moral failures and the opinions of others. After her conversation with Jesus she returned to her village differently than she left because she was free. Prior to her dialogue with Jesus, she would avoid conversation at all costs to avoid feeling condemned by her peers. Now she was initiating conversation so that others would be impacted by Jesus as she was. Perhaps after reading John 4 you feel that you don't identify with a woman of mixed Jewish and Gentile lineage who was married five times and walked in the heat of the day by herself to retrieve water. Very few, if anyone, on the planet can identify with all three of these characteristics.

However, when it comes to feeling burdened down by past failures and the opinions of others, if we are honest with ourselves in this manner, I believe that we can all relate to this social outcast whose sole intent was to travel to Jacob's well to retrieve water that would last for the day. Instead, an unexpected interaction with Jesus transformed her perspective, her life, her village and ultimately her eternity.

Everybody has a story. Liu Zhenying knows firsthand what it means to "suffer for the sake of righteousness" (I Peter 3:14). Beginning in 1949, persecution against Christians was widespread throughout China, and, by 1958, the government had successfully closed all visible churches. In that same year, Zhenying, who is more commonly referred to as Brother Yun, was born in a farming village in the southern part of China's Henan Province. AA Despite the circumstances he was born into, Brother Yun's calling was not to cultivate the soil to grow and harvest wheat, but rather preach and teach the Gospel under a communist regime. Subsequently, Brother Yun would be imprisoned and tortured, and he showed himself to be likeminded with the Apostle Paul in that being imprisoned is an opportunity to spread the Gospel to those forsaken and castoff by society. During one of his imprisonments, Brother Yun was given the responsibility, along with other individuals in the cell, to look after a prisoner until his day of execution. The prisoner Huang, was raised in a successful Chinese family but he disgraced his family's name and became a gang member, murderer, thief, and rapist. After failing to commit suicide by his own hand rather than be executed, Huang was shown the love of Jesus Christ by Brother Yun and his fellow Christian inmates. Huang broke down after being the beneficiary of undeserved love, and he received Jesus Christ as his Savior. After being baptized two days before his execution by having water dumped on his head while in a prison cell, Huang mustered up the courage to reach out one last time to two people whom he was previously too ashamed-his parents. Shortly before he was executed, Huang wrote a letter to his father and mother apologizing for dishonoring his family. Huang may have been a murderer, but God performed an amazing work in his life, and, before his death, Huang took on the role of an evangelist by sharing with his parents the hope that he found through Jesus Christ.

Still, you may be reading this and conclude you share no similarities with a Samaritan woman who lived millenniums ago and failed in marriage after marriage after marriage. Or a 22-year-old Chinese prisoner on death row for being a murder and rapist, among other things; yet, I remind you that everybody has a story. While I was working on this chapter of the book, I took a break and was cleaning out our attic when I found my speech folder from elementary school. My mother has a tendency to hold onto things for absolutely no good reason, and I have carried on this family tradition. My wife holds the viewpoint that this tradition, along with tons of useless stuff in the attic, is worth letting go. My elementary speech folder revealed a startling similarity between myself, a Samaritan woman, and a Chinese prisoner on death row. When I was taking an education class I used this folder as part of my presentation. Before I started taking speech, I was a little bit of an outgoing kid. I enjoyed talking to people, particularly those older than me. I think I would be described as socially mature for a five-year-old. Then, it became apparent that I was struggling with my pronunciation of some of my words, and I was too old for it to be considered "cute," so I needed extra help. While I didn't mind the extra help, the mocking and teasing of my classmates crushed me. I would go in our backyard and kick a soccer ball and try to say words properly. It sounded wrong to me, and I felt that it must have sounded worse to anyone else. Naturally, I didn't talk a whole lot to people outside of my circle, and I went from outgoing to shy. My struggles with speech pronunciation lasted at most a few years, but the effects socially lasted years longer. Once you are characterized a certain way, and the psychological scars of past failures and hurt stay with you, it is really hard to break free. This was true of me, this was true of a 22-year-old Chinese prisoner named Huang, and this was true of a Samaritan woman nearly 2,000 years ago who would rather face the scorching heat of the midday sun then the scorching insults of the other women in the village. How the three of us changed is as similar as our circumstances are different. We were changed by Jesus.

As I became a young adult, my walk with Jesus grew stronger and produced a confidence that occurred entirely because of the work of Jesus in my life. Looking at my speech folder and reading sentences where practically every word began with an "S," it's humbling to think how God has used me. I have preached at many churches, in addition to the church where I have the privilege to serve, I am a social studies teacher, Bible study leader, I have been the keynote speaker at a graduation, entrusted with officiating weddings, awards programs, special events, and represented people in front of politicians along with many other platforms. I say this in all humility because, of all my friends, I was the only one who needed speech tutoring, and, for some reason, God chose to use me in these areas. After graduating college, I was part of a young adult ministry. After serving alongside the pastor who oversaw this ministry, I shared with him that when I was younger, I was on the shy side, and he said, "John, I am not saying that isn't true, but I just can't picture that." All I can say is my confidence in every avenue of my life is stronger due to my relationship with Jesus Christ. For the Samaritan woman, the confidence to go into her village and boldly proclaim to them what she saw and heard was due to her interaction with Jesus. For Huang, the boldness to write to his parents after he had shamed the family name occurred because he experienced the grace of God.

How about you? Struggling to grow in certain areas of your life due to past failures and the opinions of others is commonplace. Are there areas in your life you feel incapable of growing due to failing to live up to certain standards or the opinions of others? If so, you're not alone, and you would probably be surprised how many people struggle in the same way. As we saw with the Samaritan woman, His love for you isn't based on lack of knowledge of your weaknesses and failures. God loves you despite them, and He shows His love and power by helping you overcome them. Opinions of others toward you matter far less than the opinion Jesus has of you, and your limitations matter little to a limitless God. Let Jesus be your confidence; it will transform your life.

Chapter 7 Footnotes

[1] Perhaps Galileans decision to travel through Samaria was in part due to the fact that if they were to observe the religious festivals on a regular basis they would need to travel to Jerusalem multiple times per year. Most Judeans would rarely need to travel to Galilee. On the rare occurrence that this was necessary it was easier to justify taking the long route and avoiding Samaria altogether. Josephus makes mention that Galileans would often travel through Samaria when he writes, "It was the custom of the Galileans, when they came to the holy city at the festivals, to take their journeys through the country of the Samaritans" [E]

[2] This was about 931 B.C. [F]

[3] One of the great archaeological discoveries that support the Bible is the discovery of the Black Obelisk of Shalmaneser III which depicts Jehu, the Northern King of Israel paying tribute to Shalmaneser III. [G]

[4] Hoshea ruled from 732-722 B.C. [I] II Kings 17:6 states that, "In the ninth year of Assyria, the king of Assyria captured Samaria and deported the Israelites to Assyria." Scripture doesn't specify the name of the king. We know Shalmaneser V, who ruled from 726-722 B.C. had a three-year siege on Samaria and was overthrown by Sargon II who ruled from 722-705 B.C. Sargon II claimed credit for defeating Samaria in one of his annalistic reports when he stated, "I besieged and conquered Samaria, led away as booty 27,290 inhabitants of it. I formed from them a contingent of 50 chariots and made the remaining inhabitants assume their social positions." [J] This does not necessarily mean that Sargon II was the one who defeated Samaria, as many rulers throughout history have claimed credit for the accomplishments of their predecessors. Perhaps after Shalmaneser V defeated the Samarians he was overthrown by Sargon II and he oversaw those who were exiled as well as the leadership that was installed over the region of Samaria. This shows us another example where historical records match up with the accuracy of the Biblical account.

[5] Josephus describes how Alexander the Great went into Jerusaelm. After being greeted so favorably and then marching into Jerusalem he was shown the book of Daniel and the prophecy that one of the Greeks should destroy the Persian Empire. Alexander believed he was the fulfillment of this prophecy. [L] Daniel 8:1-8 describes a ram with two horns. This ram is symbolic of Persia and the two horns are the kings of Media and Persia. Next is a male goat who is symbolic of Greece and has one horn which is symbolic of one ruler, who is Alexander the Great. [M] The goat defeats the ram just like Alexander and Greece defeat Persia in 333 B.C. [N] Daniel 8:8- "The goat became very great, but at the height of his power his large horn was broken off and in its place four prominent horns grew up toward

the four winds of heaven." This verse prophesies of the untimely death of Alexander the Great in 323 B.C. and the four horns represent that his kingdom would be split in four after his death.

[6] The priests asked Alexander the Great to allow them to be under the law of their forefathers and be allowed not to pay tribute on the seventh year. Alexander granted both of these requests and stated the Jews living in Babylon and Media would also be allowed to follow the laws of their forefathers. Alexander had many Jews join his army as he continued on his conquests. [O]

[7] Josephus described the mentality of the Samaritans by saying, "Samaritans, as we have already elsewhere declared, that when the Jews are in adversity they deny that they are of kin to them, and when they confess the truth; but when they perceive that some good fortune hath befallen, they immediately pretend to have communion with them, saying that they belong to them, and derive their genealogy from Joseph, Ephraim, and Manasseh." [P]

[8] We read in John 4:6, "Jesus, tired as He was from the journey." The Greek verb used for tired is *kopiao* which means, "to grow weary, toil." The miraculous events in Jesus' ministry it describes His Divinity. The fact that Jesus becomes weary emphasizes His humanity. Jesus appears to be more tired than His disciples as a result of the journey. This description is not showing Jesus to be weaker physically but rather the burden of His ministry was far more taxing than what was demanded of the disciples or anyone else. Jesus exhaustion was due in part to the continual opposition He was facing.

[9] Also translated, "God the God of Israel."

[10] For our calendar it would be early May [Q]

[11] The Gospel of John doesn't give us details pertaining to her age or personal appearance, we can reasonably presume a few things. If the Apostle John was the youngest and possibly even a teenager when he started following Jesus then a woman who had already been married five times would in all likelihood be significantly older than John. Additionally, as a woman of low morals, since she had no virtue to offer a man in a relationship, what she offered was physical, particularly to those who were also willing to compromise their own morals.

[12] In John 4:6 the noun used for well is *pege* which means, "a fountain, spring, well." This describes the well as not merely being still water but actually a spring that flows underground into the well.

[13] When Henry Maundrell visited Jacob's well in the late 17th century he reported that the well had 15 feet of water and was 105 feet deep. Other reports have the well at 66 feet deep. [R] Other reports give verifying statistics but the depth of the well was significant and if you didn't have any tools to draw water you would remain thirsty.

[14] Generations of Samaritans would come to this well for refreshment and reminisce about their ancestor Jacob who drank water from the same well. After hearing that stated he could offer something better, "living water" the woman openly asked, "Are you greater than our father Jacob?" The adjective used for greater is *meizon* which means, "elder, greater, more." Jews and Samaritans both used ancestry and lineage as a measuring stick for greatness. Jacob was from days of ancient past and Jews and Samaritans both held him in high regard as they were his descendants. Part of Jacob's esteem among his descendants was due to respect shown to your ancestors. The further back the greater respect. The Samaritan woman didn't realize the validity of her question because one of the enlightening truths of Scripture is that Jesus is eternal. The Apostle John begins his Gospel describing the eternal characteristics of Jesus (John 1:1). The Apostle Paul states that Jesus is before all things and holds them together (Colossians 1:17). Jesus personally stated to the religious leaders that He was before Abraham (John 8:58) and when the Apostle John was old, lonely, and exiled on Patmos Jesus appeared in His Glory to John and stated that He is, "the Alpha and Omega" (Revelation 1:8), "First and the Last" (Revelation 1:17) and "the Living One" "alive for ever and ever" (Revelation 1:18).

[15] Jeremiah wrote two books of prophecy (Jeremiah and Lamentations). Altogether there are 17 books of prophecy with five books of Major Prophets and 12 books of Minor Prophets. By not accepting the books of Scripture besides the Torah the Samaritans limited their knowledge of the Revelation found in the Word of God. Still the Messiah was prophesied in the books of Moses and no doubt many Samaritans were eager for his arrival.

[16] Scripture repeatedly expresses the benefits of flowing water rather than water which is stagnant. When the children of Israel were walking through the wilderness of Shur the water that they came to was bitter (Exodus 15:22). While God miraculously allowed the water to become sweet they found true refreshment at Elim where there was twelve springs of water and seventy palm trees (Exodus 15:27). When a man has an unclean discharge come from his body in order to be cleansed he was commanded to wash himself in flowing water (Leviticus 15:13). Flowing water provides greater refreshment and cleansing. Jesus offered "flowing water" that would spring up eternal life.

[17] The Samaritans built their own Temple around the middle of the 5th century B.C. which is around the time of Ezra and Nehemiah. [T] During the Maccabean Period which lasted from 167-63 B.C., Judea had a brief time of political independence (143-63 B.C.). [U] The Hasmoneans were rulers who emerged during this period. The first of these rulers was Simon who was appointed high priest, military commander and civil ruler

in 142 B.C. His reign came to an untimely end as a result of being assassinated in 134 B.C. which led to his son John Hyrcannus inheriting these titles of authority from 134-103 B.C. [V] After his father and brothers were murdered, and facing a challenging siege from the Seleucid Empire early on in his rule. After the death of Antiochus VII of the Seleucid Empire, with whom Hyrcannus made a treaty, Hyrcannus went on the offensive. This eventually included going into Samaria and destroying the Temple at Mt. Gerizim [W] which took place in 113 B.C. [X]

[18] In John 4:27 it states the disciples were "surprised." The verb that is used literally means "marveled" [Y] and this verb is often used in the Gospels particularly in reference both crowd's response to Jesus (Matthew 9:33; Mark 5:20; Luke 1:63) as well as individuals (Matthew 8:10; 27:14; Mark 15:5)

[19]John makes reference that she leaves her water jar when she returns to her village (John 4:28). There are a few logical reasons for this. For starters, if she was going to come back to the well she could have gotten her jar then. In her excitement not having the water jar would allow for her to get to the village quicker. Secondly, perhaps she left the jar with water so that she could honor the initial request of Jesus, giving Him a drink, and also provided water for Peter, Andrew, John, Philip and Nathaniel.

[20] Hebrews 11:37a states- "They were stoned; they were sawed in two" (ESV). We don't read in Scripture of an individual being sawed in two but tradition states this occurred to Isaiah during the wicked rule of Manasseh. This account was written in an apocryphon writing known as the *Ascension of Isaiah* [Z]

Citations

Preface

A. Olson, p. 25
B. Habermas & Licona, p. 54
C. Vos, p. 11
D. Holmes, p. 272
E. Richardson, p. 344
F. Tasker, p. 17
G. Pamphilius, Eusebius, Schaff, & Cushman p. 318
H. Habermas & Licona, p. 127
I. Richardson, p. 125
J. Beasley-Murray, p. 15

Chapter 1 Footnotes

A. Moule, p. 33
B. Eusebius, p. 86
C. Walton, p. 3
D. Vos, p. 11-12
E. Holmes, p. 722
F. Pink, p. 16
G. Schaff, *History of the Christian Church,* p. 350
H. Swindoll, p. 10
I. Frank, p. 244
J. *Antiquities of the Jews* 18.2, Josephus
K. Frank, p. 244
L. Youngblood, R.F., Bruce, & Harrison, p. 182
M. Packer, Tenney, and White, p. 532
N. *Antiquities of the Jews 18.2*
O. *Lacaenarum Apophthegmata* by Plutarch
P. Barclay, *The Gospel of Matthew* Volume 1-p. 19
Q. Edersheim*, The Temple-Its Ministry and Services,* p. 48
R. Youngblood, R.F., Bruce, F.F., & Harrison, R.K., p. 447
S. Tenney, p. 35
T. Josephus, *Wars of the Jews*-II.1-3
U. MacDonald, p. 1,376

Chapter 2 Footnotes

A. Edersheim, *The Life and Times of Jesus the Messiah* pg. 139
B. Packer, Tenney, & White, pg. 532

C. Packer, Tenney, & White, pg. 532
D. Wright, p. 36
E. Keller, p. 384
F. Riches, p. 16
G. Calvin, *Commentary on Matthew, Mark, Luke-Volume 1*, p. 162
H. Edersheim, *The Life and Times of Jesus the Messiah*, pg. 281
I. Josephus, *Antiquities* 18:2:2
J. Edersheim, *Life and Times of Jesus the Messiah*, pg. 244
K. Keller, pg. 384
L. Beitzel, pg. 460
M. Edersheim, *Life and Times of Jesus the Messiah*, pg. 244
N. Edersheim, *Life and Times of Jesus the Messiah*, pg. 244
O. Griffin-Jones, pg. 54
P. MacArthur, *Twelve Ordinary Men*, p. 182
Q. Keller, p. 375
R. Mackie, p. 25
S. Barclay, *The Gospel of Matthew-Volume 1*, p. 46
T. Tasker, pg. 57-58
U. Edersheim, *The Life and Times of Jesus the Messiah*, p. 283 pg. 20
V. *Antiquities of the Jews* xiii.10-5
W. MacArthur, *One Perfect Life*, p. 69
X. Riches, p. 46
Y. Eusebius, p. 86
Z. Holmes, p. 8
AA. Holmes, p. 8-9
BB. Josephus, *Wars of the Jews*-ii.8-2
CC. Josephus, *Antiquities of the Jews*- xviii.1-5
DD. Josephus, *Wars of the Jews*-ii.8-5
EE. Josephus, *Wars of the Jews*-ii.8-3
FF. Josephus, *Antiquities of the Jews*-xviii.1-5
GG. Josephus, *Antiquities of the Jews*-xiii.5-9
HH. Riches, p. 65
II. Beitzel, p. 516
JJ. Grudem, p. 397
KK. Showers, p. 6

Chapter 3 Footnotes

A. Barclay, *Gospel of Matthew*, p. 43
B. Wright p. 36
C. Kingsbury, p. 49
D. MacDonald, p. 1,210
E. Calvin, *Matthew, Mark, and Luke vol 1*, p. 167
F. Walton, p. 30

G. MacDonald, p. iii
H. Bock, *Who is Jesus?* p. 32
I. Keller, p. 375
J. MacDonald, p. 391
K. Neander, p. 114
L. Riches, p. 63
M. Bock, *who is Jesus?* p. 33
N. Aquinas, p. 10
O. Pink, p. 18
P. Bock, *who is Jesus?* p. 33
Q. Barclay, *Gospel of* Luke, p. 10
R. Edersheim, *The Temple-It's Ministry and Services at the time of Christ*, p. 83
S. MacArthur, *One Perfect Life,* p. 42
T. Calvin, *Commentary on Matthew, Mark, and Luke-Volume 1*, p. 34
U. Frank, p. 200
V. Neander, p. 49
W. *Calvin, Matthew, Mark, and Luke-Volume 1*, p. 84-85
X. Keller, p. 54-55
Y. Ferling, p. 152
Z. Ferling, p. 160
AA. Lillback, p. 206

Chapter 4 Footnotes

A. Beitzel, p. 423
B. Youngblood, p. 26
C. Packer, Tenney, & White-Volume 3, p. 185
D. Gouge & Gataker, Annotations on the Gospel according to S. Matthew CHAP. III V. 15
E. Bock, *Who is Jesus?* p. 28
F. Calvin, *Commentary on Matthew, Mark, and Luke-Volume 1*, p. 181
G. Aquinas, p. 12
H. Stott, p. 174
I. Barclay, *Gospel of Matthew volume 1*, p. 63
J. Holmes, p. 170
K. Richards, p. 119
L. Barclay, *The Gospel of Matthew,* p. 62
M. Griffith-Jones, p. 132
N. Edersheim, *The Temple* p. 44
O. Guinness, p. 137
P. Guinness, p. 137

Chapter 5 Footnotes

A. Barclay, *The Gospel of John volume 1,* p. 76-77
B. Swindoll, p. 40
C. Blomberg, *The historical reliability of John's* Gospel, p. 77
D. McGarvery, p. 101
E. Goodspeed, p. 38
F. McBirnie, p. 94
G. MacArthur, *One Perfect Life* p. 81
H. McGarvey, p. 110
I. *Twelve Ordinary Men,* MacArthur, p. 119
J. Archaeology Study Bible, 2005, p. 1,587
K. Beitzel, p. 425
L. France, p. 303
M. Blomberg, *The historical reliability of John's Gospel,* p. 83-84
N. Frank, p. 205
O. Beitzel, p. 425
P. Hoerth & McRay, p. 169
Q. Blomberg, *The historical reliability of John's* Gospel p. 82
R. Swindoll, p. 57
S. Carson, p. 169
T. MacArthur, *One Perfect Life* p. 83
U. Barclay, *Gospel of John-Volume 1,* p. 97
V. Barclay, *Gospel of John,* p. 97
W. Swindoll, p. 57
X. Packer, Tenney, White Jr., p. 296
Y. McGarvey, p. 117
Z. Kostenberger, p. 58
AA. Peterson, p. 47
BB. Edersheim, *The Temple,* p. 47
CC. Edersheim, *The Temple,* p. 47
DD. MacArthur, *One Perfect Life,* p. 85
EE. Mackie, p. 83
FF. Edersheim, *The Temple,* p. 45
GG. MacDonald, p. 1,475
HH. Josephus, *Antiquities of the Jews* xv. 11-1
II. Schaff, *History of the Christian Church A.D. 1-100,* p. 111

Chapter 6 Footnotes

A. Harrison, p. 23
B. Tenney, p. 48
C. Swindoll, p. 67
D. Barclay, *The Gospel of John Vol* 1, p. 124

E. Neander, p. 174
F. Calvin, *Commentary on John Vol 1*, p. 79
G. Barackman, p. 153
H. Wilson & Taylor, p. 208
I. Kostenberg, p. 69
J. Wood, p. 355
K. Levy, p. 27
L. Neander, p. 287
M. Beasley-Murray, p. 39-40
N. Swindoll, p. 17
O. Blomberg, *The historical reliability of John's* Gospel, p. 96
P. Carson, p. 209
Q. Carson, p. 211
R. Edersheim, *Life and Times of Jesus the Messiah*, p. 400

Chapter 7 Footnotes

A. MacDonald, p. 1,482
B. Carson, p. 215
C. Packer, J.I., Tenney, M.C., & White-Volume 1, p. 201
D. Beitzel, p. 319
E. Josephus, *Antiquities of the Jews* xx.vi-1
F. Walton, John H. p. 30
G. Unger, p. 250
H. MacDonald, p. 411
I. Walton, John H. p. 30
J. Hoerth & McRay, p. 53
K. Josephus, *Antiquities of the* Jews xi.viii-6
L. Josephus, *Antiquities of the* Jews xi.viii-5
M. MacDonald, p. 401
N. Keller, p. 337
O. Josephus, *Antiquities of the* Jews xi.viii-5
P. Josephus, *Antiquities of the* Jews xi.viii-6
Q. Swindoll, p. 87
R. McGarvey, p. 142
S. Kostenberger, p. 73
T. Hoerth & McRay, p. 178
U. Harrison, p. 8-9
V. Pritchard, p. 148
W. Josephus, *Antiquities of the Jews* xiii.ix-1
X. Hoerth & McRay, p. 178
Y. Blomberg, *The historical reliability of John's Gospel,* p. 102
Z. FF Bruce, p. 340
AA. Hattaway, p. 17

Bibliography

Aquinas, Thomas & translated Whiston, William (1842) *Catena Aurea-Gospel of Mark*. London, England. J.G.F. and J. Rivington (Publisher-Grand Rapids, MI: Christian Classics Ethereal Library)

Barclay, William (1975) *The Gospel of Matthew-Volume 1* (Revised Edition). Philadelphia, PA: Westminster Press. ISBN: 0-664-24100-X

Barclay, William (1975) *The Gospel of Luke* (Revised Edition). Philadelphia, PA: Westminster Press. ISBN: 0-664-24103-4

Beasley-Murray, G.R. (1991) *Gospel of Life-Theology in the Fourth Gospel*. Peabody, MA: Hendrickson Publishers, Inc. ISBN: 0-943575-76-1

Beitzel, Barry J. (2008) *Biblical-The Bible Atlas-A Social and Historical Journey Through the Lands of the Bible (2nd ed.)*. Hauppauge, NY: Barons Educational Series, Inc. ISBN: 13: 978-0-7641-6085-1

Bock, Darrell (2012) *Who is Jesus? Linking the historical Jesus with the Christ of Faith*. New York, NY. Howard Books. ISBN: 978-1-4391-9068-5

Calvin, John (1563). Translated Pringle, William. *Commentary on a Harmony of the Evangelists-Matthew, Mark, and Luke Volume One*. (1845) Grand Rapids, MI: Classic Christian Ethereal Library

Edersheim, Alfred (1883 initially written) *The Life and Times of Jesus the Messiah*. Grand Rapids, MI. Christian Classics Ethereal Library.

Edersheim, Alfred (1987 Reprinted) *The Temple-Its Ministry and Services as they were at the time of Christ*. Grand Rapids, Michigan WM. B. Eerdmans Publishing Company ISBN: 0-8028-8133-5

Eusebius. (Translated by C.F. Cruse) (Reprinted 1998) *Eusebius' Ecclesiastical History*. Peabody, MA. Hendrickson Publishers, Inc. ISBN: 13: 978-1-56563-813-6

Ferling, John (2009) *The Ascent of George Washington-The Hidden Political Genius of an American Icon*. New York, NY. Bloomsbury Press. ISBN: 978-1-60819-095-9

Frank, Harry Thomas (1975) *Discovering the Biblical World.*
Maplewood, NJ: Hammond Incorporated. ISBN: 0-06-063014-0

Griffith-Jones, Robin (2000) *The Four Witnesses-The Rebel, the Rabbi, the Chronicler, and the Mystic.* New York, NY: HarperCollins Publishers, Inc. ISBN: 0-06-251647-7

Grudem, Wayne (1994) *Systematic Theology-An Introduction to Biblical Doctrine.* Grand Rapids, MI. Zondervan. ISBN: 978-0-310-28670-7

Habermas, Gary R. & Licona, Michael R. (2004) *The Case For The Resurrection of Jesus.* Grand Rapids, MI. Kregel Publications: ISBN: 978-0-8254-2788-6

Holmes, Michael W. (2007) *The Apostolic Fathers-Greek Texts and English Translations* (3rd end). Grand Rapids, MI. Baker Academic: ISBN: 978-0-8010-3468-8

Josephus, Flavius (Translated by William Whiston) (Reprinted 1981) *The Complete Works of Josephus.* Grand Rapids, MI: Kregel Publications. ISBN: 0-8254-2952-8

Keller, Werner (1980) *The Bible as History.* New York, NY: Bantam Books. ISBN: 0-553-27943-2

Kingsbury, Jack Dean (1989) *Matthew-Structure, Christology, Kingdom.* Minneapolis, MN: Fortress Press. ISBN: 0-8006-0434-2

Lillback, Peter A. & Newcombe, Jerry (2006) *George Washington's Sacred Fire.* Bryn Mawr, PA. Providence Forum Press. ISBN: 0-9786052-6-8

MacArthur, John (2002) *Twelve Ordinary Men-How the Master Shaped His Disciples for Greatness, and What He Wants to Do with You.* Nashville, TN: Thomas Nelson Publishers. ISBN: 978-0-7852-8824-4

MacArthur, John (2012) *One Perfect Life-The Complete Story of the LORD Jesus.* Nashville, TN: Thomas Nelson Publishers. ISBN: 978-1-4016-7632-2

MacDonald, William & Farstad, Art (1995) *Believer's Bible Commentary.* Nashville, TN. Thomas Nelson Publishers. ISBN: 0-8407-1972-8

MacKie, George M. *Bible* (1898) *Bible Manners and Customs.* New York, NY. Fleming H. Revell Company.

Moule, Horace (1860) *The Roman Republic Being a Review of some of Its Salient Points In History.* London, England. Bradbury & Evans, Printers, Whitefriars

Neander, Augustus (1845) *The Life of Jesus Christ in its Historical Connexion and Historical Development 4th ed.* Grand Rapids, MI: Classical Christian Ethereal Library. (4th edition was published in 1845)

Olson, R.E. (1999) *The Story of Christian Theology: twenty centuries of tradition and reform.* Downers Grove, IL: Intervarsity Press. ISBN: 978-08303815050

Packer, J.I., Tenney, M.C., & White, W. (1995) *Illustrated Encyclopedia of Bible Facts: Volume 1: The Land and the People* Baltimore, Maryland.: Thomas Nelson Publishers, Published by Halo Press

Packer, J.I., Tenney, Merrill C., White Jr., William (1995) *Nelson's Illustrated Encyclopedia of Bible Facts Volume 3: New Testament Times.* Baltimore, MD: Halo Press.

Pamphilius, Eusebius, Schaff, Philip, & Cushman, Arthur (1885 original printing) *Nicene and Post Nicene Fathers-Series II Volume I.* Grand Rapids, MI. Christian Classics Ethereal Library. NPNF2-01

Pink, Arthur W. (1921) *Why Four Gospels?* Swengel, PA: Bible Truth Depot

Plutarch *Lacaenarum Apophthegmata.* Loeb Classical Library Edition Volume III (1931)

Richardson, Cyril C. (1970) *Early Christian Fathers.* New York, NY: Macmillan Publishing Co., Inc. ISBN: 0-02-088980-1

Riches, John (1995) *The World of Jesus-First Century Judaism in Crisis* (4th ed) New York, NY: Cambridge University Press. ISBN: 0-521-38676-4

Schaff, Philip (1882 initially written) *History of the Christian Church, Volume I: Apostolic Christianity A.D. 1-100.* Grand Rapids, MI: Classic Christian Ethereal Library

Showers, Renald (2007) *Those Invisible Spirits Called Angels* (3rd ed.) Bellmawr, NJ: The Friends of Israel Gospel Ministry, Inc. ISBN: 13: 978-0-915540-24-2

Swindoll, Charles (2010) *Swindoll's New Testament Insights-Insights on John*. Grand Rapids, MI: Zondervan: ISBN: 978-0-310-28435-2

Tasker, R.V.G. (1983) *The Gospel According to St. John* (2nd end) Grand Rapids, MI: William B. Eerdmans Publishing Company. ISBN: 0-8028-1403-4

Tenney, Merrill C. (1978) *New Testament Survey* (15th end) Grand Rapids, MI: William B. Eerdmans Publishing Company. ISBN: 0-8028-3251-2

Vos, Howard F. (1994) *Exploring Church History*. Nashville, TN: Thomas Nelson Publishers. ISBN: 0-7852-1144-6

Walton, John H. (1994) *Chronological and Background Charts of the Old Testament-Revised and Expanded Edition*. Grand Rapids, MI: Zondervan Publishing House: ISBN: 0-310-48161-9

Wright, N.T. (1999) *The Challenge of Jesus-Rediscovering Who Jesus Was and Is*. Downers Grove, IL. IVP Academic: ISBN: 10- 0-8308-2200-3

Youngblood, R.F., Bruce, F.F., & Harrison, R.K. (1995) *Nelson's New Illustrated Bible Dictionary* (2nd ed.) Nashville, TN: Thomas Nelson Publishers. ISBN: 0-8407-2071-8

Made in the USA
Columbia, SC
25 November 2018